PRAISE FOR

Same as Ever

"Want to understand the changing world? Start with what stays the same. That's the amazing conclusion of Morgan Housel's fascinating, useful, and highly-entertaining book."

—ARTHUR C. BROOKS

Professor, Harvard Kennedy School and Harvard Business School, and #1 *New York Times* bestselling author

"Morgan Housel has done it again. *Same as Ever* brims with wisdom and wit, and Housel has an ingenious way of selecting the perfect, unforgettable story to drive home timeless lessons about money, life, storytelling, ambition, and satisfaction. This little book contains a library's worth of wisdom."

—DEREK THOMPSON

The Atlantic

"This book is both profoundly thoughtful, almost impossible to put down, and really important. Housel explains how so much of what determines our fate is random, seemingly hanging from a thread—and yet, there are also universal truths that have stayed consistent over centuries. What Housel shows is how to find them."

—BETHANY MCLEAN

Bestselling coauthor of *The Smartest Guys in the Room* and *All the Devils are Here*

"Life-changing insights from a fantastic story teller."

—RYAN HOLIDAY

Bestselling author of *The Obstacle is the Way* and *The Daily Dad*

"*The Psychology of Money* is a fast-paced, engaging read that will leave you with both the knowledge to understand why we make bad financial decisions and the tools to make better ones."

—ANNIE DUKE

Author, *Thinking in Bets*

"I've recommended it to a lot of friends and I don't do that lightly. There is a reputational risk. Books take some time to read. So I generally will withhold my recommendations, unless I am absolutely sure. But the reframing and the perspectives and the hypotheticals and the thought exercises ... I find to be very powerful."

—TIM FERRISS

Author of five #1 *NYT/WSJ* bestsellers, investor, and host of *The Tim Ferriss Show* podcast

"Housel's observations often hit the daily double: they say things that haven't been said before, and they make sense."

—HOWARD MARKS

Director and Co-Chairman, Oaktree Capital and author, *The Most Important Thing* and *Mastering the Market Cycle*

"He is accessible to everyone wanting to learn more about the psychology of money. I highly recommend this book."

—JAMES P. O'SHAUGHNESSY

Author, *What Works on Wall Street*

"Few people write about finance with the graceful clarity of Morgan Housel. *The Psychology of Money* is an essential read for anyone who wants to make wiser decisions or live a richer life."

—DANIEL H. PINK

#1 *New York Times* bestselling author of *The Power of Regret*, *When*, *To Sell is Human*, and *Drive*

"There aren't a lot of people on my must-read list. Morgan is certainly one of them. ... He could be the most popular writer in finance today."

—BARRY RITHOLTZ

Bloomberg Radio, *Masters in Business*

"[Housel] writes beautifully and wisely about a central truth: Money isn't primarily a store of value. Money is a conduit of emotion and ego, carrying hopes and fears, dreams and heartbreak, confidence and surprise, envy and regret."

—JASON ZWEIG

Wall Street Journal

Same as Ever

Same as Ever

Ever

TIMELESS LESSONS ON RISK,
OPPORTUNITY, AND LIVING A GOOD LIFE

MORGAN HOUSEL

Harriman
House

HARRIMAN HOUSE LTD
3 Viceroy Court
Bedford Road
Petersfield
Hampshire
GU32 3LJ
GREAT BRITAIN
Tel: +44 (0)1730 233870

Email: enquiries@harriman-house.com
Website: harriman.house

First published in 2023.
Copyright © Morgan Housel
Published by arrangement with the Portfolio, an imprint of Penguin Publishing Group, a division of Penguin Random House LLC.

The right of Morgan Housel to be identified as the Author has been asserted in accordance with the Copyright, Design and Patents Act 1988.

Paperback ISBN: 978-1-80409-094-7
eBook ISBN: 978-1-80409-064-0

British Library Cataloguing in Publication Data
A CIP catalogue record for this book can be obtained from the British Library.

Only for sale in the Indian subcontinent.

Printed and bound in India by Replika Press Pvt. Ltd.

For the reasonable optimists

Our life is indeed the same as it ever was. . . . The same physiological and psychological processes that have been man's for hundreds of thousands of years still endure.

—Carl Jung

The wise in all ages have always said the same thing, and the fools, who at all times form the immense majority, have in their way, too, acted alike, and done just the opposite.

—Arthur Schopenhauer

History never repeats itself; man always does.

—Voltaire

I've learned an important trick: to develop foresight, you need to practice hindsight.

—Jane McGonigal

The dead outnumber the living . . . fourteen to one, and we ignore the accumulated experience of such a huge majority of mankind at our peril.

—Niall Ferguson

23 Little Stories about Things That Never Change

Incentives: The Most Powerful Force in the World

When the incentives are crazy, the behavior is crazy. People can be led to justify and defend nearly anything.

Now You Get It

Nothing is more persuasive than what you've experienced firsthand.

Time Horizons

Saying "I'm in it for the long run" is a bit like standing at the base of Mount Everest, pointing to the top, and saying, "That's where I'm heading." Well, that's nice. Now comes the test.

Trying Too Hard

There are no points awarded for difficulty.

Wounds Heal, Scars Last

What have you experienced that I haven't that makes you believe what you do? And would I think about the world like you do if I experienced what you have?

Introduction

The Little Laws of Life.

I ONCE HAD LUNCH with a guy who's close to Warren Buffett. This guy—we'll call him Jim (not his real name)—was driving around Omaha, Nebraska, with Buffett in late 2009. The global economy was crippled at this point, and Omaha was no exception. Stores were closed, businesses were boarded up.

Jim said to Warren, "It's so bad right now. How does the economy ever bounce back from this?"

Warren said, "Jim, do you know what the bestselling candy bar was in 1962?"

"No," Jim said.

"Snickers," said Warren. "And do you know what the bestselling candy bar is today?"

"No," said Jim.

"Snickers," Warren said.

Then silence. That was the end of the conversation.

This is a book of short stories about what never changes in a changing world.

History is filled with surprises no one could have seen coming. But it's also filled with so much timeless wisdom.

If you traveled in time to five hundred years ago or five hundred years from now, you would be astounded at how much technology and medicine has changed. The geopolitical order would make no sense to you. The language and dialect might be completely foreign.

But you'd notice people falling for greed and fear just like they do in our current world.

You'd see people persuaded by risk, jealousy, and tribal affiliations in ways that are familiar to you.

You'd see overconfidence and shortsightedness that remind you of people's behavior today.

You'd find people seeking the secret to a happy life and trying to find certainty when none exists in ways that are entirely relatable.

When transported to an unfamiliar world, you'd spend a few minutes watching people behave and say, "Ah. I've seen this before. Same as ever."

Change captures our attention because it's surprising and exciting. But the behaviors that never change are history's most powerful lessons, because they preview what to expect in the future. Your future. *Everyone's future.* No matter who you are, where you're from, how old you are, or how much money you make, there are timeless lessons from human behavior that are some of the most important things you can ever learn.

It's a simple idea, but it's so easy to overlook. And once you grasp it, you'll be able to make better sense of your own life, understand why the world is the way it is, and become more at ease with what the future has in store.

Amazon founder Jeff Bezos once said that he's often asked what's going to change in the next ten years. "I almost never get the question: 'What's not going to change in the next ten years?'"

he said. "And I submit to you that that second question is actually the more important of the two."

Things that never change are important because you can put so much confidence into knowing how they'll shape the future. Bezos said it's impossible to imagine a future where Amazon customers don't want low prices and fast shipping—so he can put enormous investment into those things.

The same philosophy works in almost all areas of life.

I have no clue what the stock market will do next year (or any year). But I'm very confident about people's penchant for greed and fear, which never changes. So that's what I spend my time thinking about.

I have no idea who will win the next presidential election. But I'm confident about the ways people's attachment to tribal identities influences their thinking, which is the same today as it was a thousand years ago and will be a thousand years from now.

I cannot tell you what businesses will dominate the next decade. But I can tell you how business leaders let success go to their heads, becoming lazy and entitled and eventually losing their edge. That story hasn't changed in hundreds of years and never will.

Philosophers have spent centuries discussing the idea that there are an infinite number of ways your life could play out, and you just happen to be living in this specific version. It's a wild thing to contemplate, and it leads to the question: What would be true in *every imaginable* version of your life, not just this one? Those universal truths are obviously the most important things to focus on, because they don't rely on chance, luck, or accident.

Entrepreneur and investor Naval Ravikant put it this way: "In 1,000 parallel universes, you want to be wealthy in 999 of them. You don't want to be wealthy in the fifty of them where you got lucky, so we want to factor luck out of it. . . . I want to live in a way that if my life played out 1,000 times, Naval is successful 999 times."

That's what this book is about: In a thousand parallel universes, what would be true in every single one?

Each of the following twenty-three chapters can be read independently, so there is no harm in skipping and choosing as you wish. What they have in common is that I'm confident each of these topics will be as relevant hundreds of years from now as they were hundreds of years ago.

None of the chapters are long, and you're welcome for that. Many are derived from my blog at the Collaborative Fund, where I write about the intersection of money, history, and psychology.

The first looks at how fragile the world is, with a personal story about the scariest day of my life.

Hanging by a Thread

If you know where we've been,
you realize we have no idea
where we're going.

A BIG LESSON FROM history is realizing how much of the world hangs by a thread. Some of the biggest and most consequential changes in history happened because of a random, unforeseeable, thoughtless encounter or decision that led to magic or mayhem.

Author Tim Urban once wrote, "If you went back in time before your birth you'd be terrified to do anything, because you'd know that even the smallest nudges to the present can have major impacts on the future."

How hauntingly true.

Let me tell you a personal story about how I became interested in this topic.

I grew up ski racing in Lake Tahoe. I was on the Squaw Valley Ski Team, and it was the center of my life for a decade.

Our ski team consisted of a dozen racers. By the early 2000s we were teenagers, and most of us had spent the majority of our lives together. We skied six days a week, ten months a year, traveling the globe to wherever we could find snow.

I wasn't close to most of them—we spent too much time together and fought like cats. But four of us had become inseparable friends. This is the story of two of those friends—Brendan Allan and Bryan Richmond.

On February 15, 2001, our team had just returned from a race in Colorado. Our flight home was delayed because Lake Tahoe had been hit with a blizzard extreme even by its own standards.

You can't ski race when there's a blanket of new snow—racing requires hard-packed ice. So training was canceled, and Brendan, Bryan, and I prepared for a week of what we called free skiing: unstructured goofing off, skiing around, and having a good time.

Earlier that month Tahoe received several feet of light, fluffy snow that comes from bitter-cold air. The storm that hit in mid-February was different. It was warm—barely at the freezing point—and powerful, leaving three feet of heavy, wet snow.

We didn't think about it at the time, but the combination of heavy snow on top of fluffy snow creates textbook avalanche conditions. A light base of snow with a heavy layer on top is incredibly fragile and prone to sliding.

Ski resorts are pretty good at protecting customers from avalanches by closing off the most dangerous slopes and using explosives to intentionally set off avalanches late at night, before customers arrive in the morning.

But if you're skiing out of bounds—ducking under the DO NOT CROSS ropes to ski the forbidden, untouched terrain—that system won't help you.

On the morning of February 21, 2001, Brendan, Bryan, and

I met in the Squaw Valley Ski Team locker room, like we had hundreds of times before. Bryan's last words when he left his house that morning were, "Don't worry, Mom, I won't ski out of bounds."

But as soon as we clicked into our skis, that's what we did.

The backside of Squaw Valley (now called Palisades Tahoe), behind the KT-22 chairlift, is a stretch of mountain about a mile long that separates Squaw from Alpine Meadows ski resort.

It's amazing skiing—steep and wide-open, with rolling terrain.

Before February 21 I had skied it maybe a dozen times. It wasn't one of our frequent spots, because it takes so much time. It spits you out on a backcountry road, from where we would hitchhike back to our locker room.

Brendan, Bryan, and I decided to ski it that morning.

Within seconds of ducking under the out-of-bounds ropes, I remember getting caught in an avalanche.

I had never experienced one before, but it was unforgettable. I didn't hear or see the slide. I just suddenly realized my skis weren't on the ground anymore—I was literally floating in a cloud of snow. You have no control in these situations, because rather than you pushing the snow to gain traction with your skis, the snow is pushing you. The best you can do is keep your balance to remain upright.

The avalanche was small, and ended quickly.

"Did you see that avalanche?" I remember saying when we got to the road.

"Haha, that was awesome," Brendan said.

We didn't say another word about it as we hitchhiked back to our locker room.

When we got back to Squaw, Brendan and Bryan said they wanted to ski the backside again.

I don't know why, but I didn't want to go.

But I had an idea. Brendan and Bryan could ski the backside again, and I would drive around and pick them up so they wouldn't have to hitchhike back.

We agreed on the plan and went our separate ways.

Thirty minutes later I drove to the backcountry road where I was scheduled to pick up Brendan and Bryan.

They weren't there.

I waited another thirty minutes before giving up. It took about a minute to ski down, so I knew they weren't coming. I figured they had beat me to the bottom and already hitchhiked back.

I drove back to our locker room, expecting to find them. They weren't there either. I asked around. No one had seen them.

Later that day, around 4:00 p.m., Bryan's mom called me at home. I remember every word.

"Hi, Morgan, Bryan didn't show up for work today. Do you know where he is?" she asked.

I told her the truth. "We skied the backside of KT-22 this morning. He and Brendan did it again, I was going to pick them up on the road. But they weren't there, and I haven't seen them since."

"Oh my God," she said. Click.

Bryan's mom was an expert skier herself. I think in that moment she pieced together what may have happened. I did too.

The hours ticked by, and everyone started to worry.

Someone eventually called the police and filed a missing person report. The police didn't take it very seriously, suggesting Brendan and Bryan likely snuck off to a party.

I knew that was wrong. "Their shoes are right there," I said, pointing to Brendan's and Bryan's sneakers on the locker-room floor. "That means their ski boots are on their feet. And it's now

9:00 p.m. Think about that. It's 9:00 p.m. and they have their ski boots on their feet." It was the first moment everyone looked around and realized how bad this was.

Around ten I was told to go to the Squaw Valley Fire Department, where I met the local search and rescue team.

I explained everything that Brendan, Bryan, and I did that day. The search team pulled out these giant photo maps that must have been taken from a helicopter. I showed them exactly where we entered the out-of-bounds area.

I told them about the small avalanche that morning. As soon as I mentioned it I could see the dots connecting in the rescuers' heads. I remember that when I finished talking two of the rescuers looked at each other and sighed.

In the middle of the night, with giant floodlights and a team of search dogs, the rescuers went looking for Brendan and Bryan.

I later learned that as soon as they entered the out-of-bounds area where I told them we skied, they discovered the fresh scars of a recent avalanche debris field. It was massive, "like half the mountain had been torn away," one said.

I drove back to the locker room around midnight. The Squaw Valley parking lot can hold several thousand cars. By this time it was almost empty. Everyone had gone home, except two cars parked next to each other: Brendan's Jeep and Bryan's Chevy pickup.

I tried to sleep on a bench in the locker room but couldn't shut my eyes. I remember thinking Brendan and Bryan would come bounding through the door, and we could laugh about the time I had to call the cops to find them.

By nine a.m. the locker room was packed with other ski racers, parents, friends, and family, all eager to help. It became a staging area for the search.

I laid back down on the bench and finally fell asleep.

A few minutes later I awoke to the sound of a scream, yelling, and commotion.

I knew what had happened. No one needed to say it.

I walked to the second floor of the locker room, where I saw Bryan's mom on a couch. The scream was hers.

"I'm so sorry," I told her, bawling.

It's hard to describe a moment like that. I didn't know what else to say then. I don't know what else to say now.

Search dogs had homed in on a spot in the avalanche field where rescuers with probe poles found Brendan and Bryan buried under six feet of snow.

They were born one day apart, and died ten feet from each other.

———

Later that day I drove to see my dad at work. I wanted to be around my family. He met me in the parking lot and said, "I've never been so happy to see you." It's the only time in my life I've seen him cry. It didn't occur to me until that moment how close I was to going with Brendan and Bryan on that fateful run.

Then I began wondering: Why did I ski the backside with them once that morning, then decline a second run—a decision that almost certainly saved my life?

I've thought about it a million times. I have no idea.

I have no idea.

There is no explanation.

I didn't think it through, I didn't calculate the danger, I didn't consult an expert, I didn't weigh the pros and cons.

It was a complete fluke, a random and thoughtless bit of dumb luck that became the most important decision of my life—far more important than every intentional decision I've ever made—or ever will make.

That's my personal story, and maybe you have a similar one

about your own life. But if you look, I think you'll see that a lot of history is the same.

Let me give you three freakish examples about how much of today's world relies on a few tiny things you'd never think about.

––––––––

The Battle of Long Island was a disaster for George Washington's army. His ten thousand troops were crushed by the British and its four-hundred-ship fleet.

But it could have been so much worse. It could have been the end of the Revolutionary War.

All the British had to do was sail up the East River and Washington's cornered troops would have been wiped out.

But it never happened, because the wind wasn't blowing in the right direction and sailing up the river became impossible.

Historian David McCullough once told interviewer Charlie Rose that "if the wind had been in the other direction on the night of August twenty-eighth [1776], I think it would have all been over."

"No United States of America if that had happened?" Rose asked.

"I don't think so," said McCullough.

"Just because of the wind, history was changed?" asked Rose.

"Absolutely," said McCullough.

––––––––

Compelled to save money, Captain William Turner shut down the fourth boiler room on his giant steamship for its passage from New York to Liverpool. The decision would slow the ship's voyage by one day—an annoyance, but worth the savings as the passenger-ship industry struggled economically.

Little did he or anyone else know how fateful the decision would be.

The delay meant Turner's ship—the *Lusitania*—would now sail directly into the path of a German submarine.

The *Lusitania* was hit with a torpedo, killing nearly twelve hundred passengers and becoming the most important trigger to rally U.S. public support for entering World War I.

Had the fourth boiler room been operating, Turner would have reached Liverpool a day before the German submarine had even entered the Celtic Sea, where it crossed paths with the *Lusitania*. The ship likely would have avoided attack. A country may have avoided a war that became the seed event for the rest of the twentieth century.

———

Giuseppe Zangara was tiny, barely five feet tall. He stood on a chair outside a Miami political rally in 1933 because that was the only way he could aim his gun across the crowd.

Zangara fired five shots. One of them hit Chicago mayor Anton Cermak, who was shaking hands with Zangara's intended target. Cermak died. The target, Franklin Delano Roosevelt, was sworn in as president two weeks later.

Within months of his inauguration Roosevelt transformed the U.S. economy through the New Deal. John Nance Garner—who would have become president had Zangara hit his target—opposed most of the New Deal's deficit spending. He almost certainly wouldn't have enacted many of the same policies, some of which still shape today's economy.

———

You can play this game all day. Every big story could have turned out differently if a few little puffs of nothingness went the other direction.

So much of the world hangs by a thread.

An irony of studying history is that we often know exactly how a story ends, but we have no idea where it began.

Here's an example: What caused the 2008 financial crisis?

Well, you have to understand the mortgage market.

What shaped the mortgage market? Well, you have to understand the thirty-year decline in interest rates that preceded it.

What caused falling interest rates? Well, you have to understand the inflation of the 1970s.

What caused that inflation? Well, you have to understand the monetary system of the 1970s and the hangover effects from the Vietnam War.

What caused the Vietnam War? Well, you have to understand the West's fear of communism after World War II . . . and so on forever.

Every current event—big or small—has parents, grandparents, great-grandparents, siblings, and cousins. Ignoring that family tree can muddy your understanding of events, giving a false impression of why things happened, how long they might last, and under what circumstances they might occur again. Viewing events in isolation, without an appreciation of their long roots, helps explain everything from why forecasting is hard to why politics is nasty.

People like to say, "To know where we're going, you have to know where we've been." But more realistic is admitting that if you know where we've been, you realize we have no idea where we're going. Events compound in unfathomable ways.

I try to keep two things in mind in a world that's this vulnerable to chance and accident.

One is highlighting this book's premise—to base predictions on how people behave rather than on specific events. Predicting what the world will look like fifty years from now is impossible. But predicting that people will still respond to greed, fear, opportunity, exploitation, risk, uncertainty, tribal affiliations, and social persuasion in the same way is a bet I'd take.

Forecasting events is hard because it's easy to skip the question "And then what?"

Saying "Higher gas prices will cause people to drive less" seems logical.

But then what?

Well, people have to drive, so maybe they'll look for more fuel-efficient vehicles. They'll complain to politicians, who will offer tax breaks to buy those vehicles. OPEC is asked to drill more; energy entrepreneurs innovate. And the oil industry knows two speeds: boom and bust. So they'll probably pump too much. Then prices fall, all while people own more efficient vehicles. Then maybe the suburbs become more popular—and people end up driving even more than before.

So who knows.

Every event creates its own offspring, which impact the world in their own special ways. It makes prediction exceedingly hard. The absurdity of past connections should humble your confidence in predicting future ones.

The other thing to keep in mind is to have a wider imagination. No matter what the world looks like today, and what seems obvious today, everything can change tomorrow because of some tiny accident no one's thinking about. Events, like money, compound. And the central feature of compounding is that it's never intuitive how big something can grow from a small beginning.

Next, let me tell you another old story showing how easy it is to ignore risks.

Risk Is What
You Don't See

We are very good at predicting the future,
except for the surprises—which tend
to be all that matter.

I'T'S WELL-KNOWN THAT people are bad at predicting the future.

But this misses an important nuance: We are very good at predicting the future, except for the surprises—which tend to be all that matter.

The biggest risk is always what no one sees coming, because if no one sees it coming, no one's prepared for it; and if no one's prepared for it, its damage will be amplified when it arrives.

A quick story about a guy who learned this the hard way.

Before launching themselves into space on rockets, NASA astronauts ran tests in high-altitude hot-air balloons.

A balloon flight on May 4, 1961, took American Victor Prather and another pilot to 113,720 feet, scraping the edge of space. The goal was to test NASA's new space suit.

The flight was a success. The suit worked beautifully.

As Prather descended back to earth, he opened the faceplate on his helmet when he was low enough to breathe on his own, ostensibly to catch some fresh air.

He landed in the ocean as planned, where a helicopter was to pull him to safety. But there was a small mishap: While connecting himself to the helicopter's rescue line, Prather slipped, falling into the ocean.

This shouldn't have been that big a deal, and no one in the rescue helicopter panicked. The space suit should have been watertight and buoyant.

But since Prather had opened his faceplate, he was now exposed to the elements. Water rushed into his suit. Prather drowned.

Think of how much planning goes into launching someone into space. So much expertise, so many contingencies. So many what-ifs and what-thens. Every detail is contemplated by thousands of experts. NASA is probably the most planning-centric organization that has ever existed; you don't go to the moon by crossing your fingers and hoping for the best. Every conceivable risk has a plan A, plan B, plan C.

But even then—despite so much planning—a tiny thing no one had considered invites catastrophe.

As financial advisor Carl Richards says, "Risk is what's left over after you think you've thought of everything."

That's the real definition of risk—what's left over after you've prepared for the risks you can imagine.

Risk is what you don't see.

Look at the big news stories that move the needle—COVID-19, 9/11, Pearl Harbor, the Great Depression. Their common trait isn't necessarily that they were big; it's that they were surprises, on virtually no one's radar until they arrived.

"After booms come busts" is about as close to economic law as it gets. Study history, and the calamity that followed the booming 1920s, late 1990s, and early 2000s seems more than obvious. It seems inevitable.

In October 1929—the peak of history's craziest stock bubble and the eve of the Great Depression—economist Irving Fisher famously told an audience that "stock prices have reached what looks like a permanently high plateau."

We look at these comments today and laugh. How could someone so smart be so blind to something so inevitable? If you follow the rule that the crazier the boom, the harder the bust, the Great Depression must have been obvious.

But Fisher was a smart guy. And he wasn't alone.

In an interview years ago I asked Robert Shiller, who won the Nobel Prize for his work on bubbles, about the inevitability of the Great Depression. He responded:

> Well, nobody forecasted that. Zero. Nobody. Now there were, of course, some guys who were saying the stock market is overpriced. But if you look at what they said, did that mean a depression is coming? A decade-long depression? No one said that.
>
> I have asked economic historians to give me the name of someone who predicted the depression, and it comes up zero.

That stuck with me. Here we are today, blessed with hindsight, knowing the crash after the Roaring Twenties was obvious and inevitable. But for those who lived through it—people for whom the 1930s was a yet-to-be-discovered future—it was anything but.

Two things can explain something that looks inevitable but wasn't predicted by those who experienced it at the time:

- Either everyone in the past was blinded by delusion.
- Or everyone in the present is fooled by hindsight.

We are crazy to think it's all the former and none of the latter.

The Economist—a magazine I admire—publishes a forecast of the year ahead each January. Its January 2020 issue does not mention a single word about COVID-19. Its January 2022 issue does not mention a single word about Russia invading Ukraine.

That's not a criticism—both events were impossible to know when the issues were planned in the months before publication.

But that's the point: The biggest news, the biggest risks, the most consequential events are always what you don't see coming.

Put another way: There is rarely more or less economic uncertainty; just changes in how ignorant people are to potential risks. Asking what the biggest risks are is like asking what you expect to be surprised about. If you knew what the biggest risk was you would do something about it, and doing something about it would make it less risky. What your imagination can't fathom is the dangerous stuff, and it's why risk can never be mastered.

I can promise you that will be the case going forward. The biggest risk and the most important news story of the next ten years will be something nobody is talking about today. No matter what year you're reading this book, that truth will remain. I can say that confidently because it's always been true. The fact that you can't see it coming is exactly what makes it risky.

Even for something as giant as the Great Depression, many people were blind to what was happening even when it was well under way.

The Depression, as we know today, began in 1929. But when the well-informed members of the National Economic League were polled in 1930 as to what they considered the biggest problem of the United States, they listed, in order:

1. Administration of justice
2. Prohibition
3. Disrespect for law
4. Crime
5. Law enforcement
6. World peace

And in *eighteenth place* . . . unemployment.

A year later, in 1931—a full two years into what we now consider the Great Depression—unemployment had moved to just fourth place, behind prohibition, justice, and law enforcement.

That's what made the Great Depression so awful: No one was prepared for it because no one saw it coming. So people couldn't deal with it financially (paying their debts) and mentally (the shock and grief of sudden loss).

A big part of this idea is coming to terms with how limited our view of what's happening in the world can be.

Franklin Delano Roosevelt looked around the room and chuckled when his presidential library opened in 1941. A reporter asked why he was so cheerful. "I'm thinking of all the historians who will come here thinking they'll find the answers to their questions," he said.

There is so much we don't know. And not just about the future, but the past.

History knows three things: 1) what's been photographed, 2) what someone wrote down or recorded, and 3) the words spoken by people whom historians and journalists wanted to interview and who agreed to be interviewed.

What percentage of everything important that's ever happened falls into one of those three categories? No one knows. But it's tiny. And all three suffer from misinterpretation, incompleteness, embellishment, lying, and selective memory.

When your view of what's happening and has happened in the world is so limited, it's easy to underestimate what you don't know, what else could be happening right now, and what could go wrong that you're not even envisioning.

Think of a content child, blissfully playing with toys and smiling as the sun hits their face.

In their mind, everything is great. Their world begins and ends with their immediate surroundings—Mom is here, Dad is there, toys are nearby, food is in my stomach. As far as they're concerned, life is perfect. They have all the information they need.

What they're unaware of is so much greater. In the mind of a three-year-old, the concept of geopolitics is completely unimaginable. The idea of rising interest rates hurting the economy, or the reason someone needs a paycheck, or what a career even is, or the risk of cancer, is utterly out of sight, out of mind.

Psychologist Daniel Kahneman says, "The idea that what you don't see might refute everything you believe just doesn't occur to us."

The wild thing is adults are just as blind to what's going on in the world.

There's a haunting video of a local New York City newscast from the morning of September 11, 2001, minutes before the terrorist attacks took place. It begins: "Good morning; sixty-four degrees at eight. It's Tuesday, September eleventh. . . . It's going to be a beautiful day today, sunshine throughout. Really a splendid September day. The afternoon temperature is about eighty degrees . . ."

Risk is what they couldn't see coming.

———

By definition there's not much you can do about this. It's one of those things that just is.

It's impossible to plan for what you can't imagine, and the more you think you've imagined everything the more shocked you'll be when something happens that you hadn't considered.

But two things can push you in a more helpful direction.

One, think of risk the way the State of California thinks of earthquakes. It knows a major earthquake will happen. But it has no idea when, where, or of what magnitude. Emergency crews are prepared despite no specific forecast. Buildings are designed to withstand earthquakes that may not occur for a century or more. Nassim Taleb says, "Invest in preparedness, not in prediction." That gets to the heart of it.

Risk is dangerous when you think it requires a specific forecast before you start preparing for it. It's better to have expectations that risk will arrive, though you don't know when or where, than to rely exclusively on forecasts—almost all of which are either nonsense or about things that are well-known. Expectations and forecasts are two different things, and in a world where risk is what you don't see, the former is more valuable than the latter.

Two, realize that if you're only preparing for the risks you can envision, you'll be unprepared for the risks you can't see every single time. So, in personal finance, the right amount of savings is when it feels like it's a little too much. It should feel excessive; it should make you wince a little.

The same goes for how much debt you think you should handle—whatever you think it is, the reality is probably a little less. Your preparation shouldn't make sense in a world where the biggest historical events all would have sounded absurd before they happened.

Most of the time, when someone's caught unprepared, it's not because they didn't plan. Sometimes it's the smartest planners in the world, working tirelessly, mapping every scenario they can imagine, who end up failing. They planned for everything that made sense before getting hit by something they'd never imagined.

Harry Houdini used to invite the strongest man in the audience onstage. Then he'd ask the man to punch him in the stomach as hard as he could.

Houdini was an amateur boxer and told crowds he could withstand any man's punch with barely a flinch. The stunt matched what people loved about his famous escapes: the idea that his body could conquer physics.

After a show in 1926 Houdini invited a group of students backstage to meet him. One, a guy named Gordon Whitehead, walked up and started punching Houdini in the stomach without warning.

Whitehead didn't mean any harm. He thought he was just re-creating the same trick he'd just seen Houdini perform.

But Houdini wasn't prepared to be punched like he would be onstage. He wasn't flexing his solar plexus, steadying his stance, and holding his breath like he normally would before the trick. Whitehead caught him off guard. Houdini waved him off, clearly suffering.

The next day Houdini woke up doubled over in pain.

His appendix was ruptured, almost certainly from Whitehead's punches.

And then Harry Houdini died.

He was probably the most talented person in history at surviving big risks. Tie him up in chains and throw him into a river? No problem. Bury him alive in sand? No issue, he could escape in seconds—because he had a plan.

But a little jab from a student that he didn't see coming and wasn't prepared for?

That was the biggest risk.

What you don't see coming always is.

Next, let's chat about our expectations, and the tragedy of a life where almost everything gets better but happiness goes nowhere.

Expectations
and Reality

The first rule of happiness
is low expectations.

YOUR HAPPINESS DEPENDS on your expectations more than
anything else. So in a world that tends to get better for most
people most of the time, an important life skill is getting the
goalpost to stop moving. It's also one of the hardest.

A common storyline of history goes like this: Things get better,
wealth increases, technology brings new efficiencies, and medicine
saves lives. The quality of life goes up. But people's expectations
then rise by just as much, if not more, because those improvements
also benefit other people around you, whose circumstances you
anchor to. Happiness is little changed despite the world improving.

It's been like this forever. Montesquieu wrote Two hundred
and seventy-five years ago, "If you only wished to be happy, this
could be easily accomplished; but we wish to be happier than

other people, and this is always difficult, for we believe others to be happier than they are."

John D. Rockefeller never had penicillin, sunscreen, or Advil. But you can't say a low-income American with Advil and sunscreen today should feel better off than Rockefeller, because that's not how people's heads work. People gauge their well-being relative to those around them, and luxuries become necessities in a remarkably short period of time when the people around you become better off.

Investor Charlie Munger once noted that the world isn't driven by greed; it's driven by envy.

Let me show you what he means, with a little story about the 1950s.

———————

"The present and immediate future seem astonishingly good," *Life* magazine's January 1953 cover story begins.

"The country has just lived through what was economically the greatest year in its history," it went on. It had done this with "10 straight years of full employment, through new management attitudes which include an increasing realization that the well-paid worker, who does his job under healthy and agreeable conditions, is a valuable worker."

Wealth came so fast to so many that it was jarring. "In the 1930s I worried about how I could eat," *Life* quotes one taxi driver. "Now I'm worrying about where to park."

If these quotes don't surprise you, it's because the 1950s are so often remembered as the golden age of middle-class prosperity. Ask Americans when the country was at its greatest and the 1950s is usually near the top. Compared to today? Different worlds, no comparison. The overwhelming feeling is: It was better then.

There is a common nostalgic vision of a typical American life in the 1950s. George Friedman, a geopolitical forecaster, once summarized:

In the 1950s and 1960s, the median income allowed you to live with a single earner—normally the husband, with the wife typically working as a homemaker—and roughly three children. It permitted the purchase of modest tract housing, one late model car and an older one. It allowed a driving vacation somewhere and, with care, some savings as well.

This version of the 1950s lifestyle is true in the sense that the median American family indeed had three kids and a dog named Spot and a breadwinning husband who worked at the factory, on and on.

But the idea that the typical family was better off then than now—that they were more prosperous and more secure, by nearly any metric—is easy to debunk.

Median family income adjusted for inflation was $29,000 in 1955. In 1965 it was $42,000. In 2021 it was $70,784.

Life described the 1950s as prosperous in a way that would have seemed unbelievable to someone living in the 1920s. The same is true today—a 1950s family would have found it unfathomable that their grandchildren would earn more than twice as much as they did.

And higher income wasn't due to working more hours, or entirely due to women joining the workforce in greater numbers. Median hourly wages adjusted for inflation are nearly 50 percent higher today than in 1955.

Some of today's economic worries would have puzzled a 1950s family.

The homeownership rate was 12 percentage points lower in 1950 than it is today.

An average home was a third smaller than today's, despite having more occupants.

Food consumed 29 percent of an average household's budget in 1950 versus 13 percent today.

Workplace deaths were three times higher than today.

That's the economic era we long for?

Yes. And it's important to understand why.

———————

Ben Ferencz had a hard childhood. His immigrant father didn't speak English, was unemployable, and settled in an area of New York controlled by the Italian mob, where violence was a part of everyday life.

But Ferencz said none of it seemed to bother his parents. They were thrilled. He recalled:

> It was a tough life but they didn't know it because where they'd come from it was tougher. So it was an improvement no matter what.

The Ferenczes fled Romania to escape Jewish persecution during the Holocaust. The family came to America on the open deck of a ship in the middle of winter, nearly freezing to death. Ferencz later became a lawyer and prosecuted Nazi war criminals during the Nuremberg trials, and he was one of the happiest people I came across.

It's staggering how expectations can alter how you interpret current circumstances.

I have a friend who grew up in abject poverty in Africa. He now works in tech in California. He says to this day he is still blown away when he eats a hot meal. It's astounding to him how abundant food is in America. And that's astounding for me to ponder—he finds immense pleasure in something I don't think twice about.

In 2007 *The New York Times* interviewed Gary Kremen, who founded Match.com. At the time, Kremen was forty-three years old and worth $10 million. That put him in the top half of 1 percent of people in the country, and probably the top one thousandth of 1 percent of people in the world. In Silicon Valley, however, it made him just another guy. "You're nobody here at $10 million," he said. The *Times* wrote: "He logs 60- to 80-hour workweeks because he does not think he has nearly enough money to ease up."

There is no such thing as objective wealth—everything is relative, and mostly relative to those around you. It's the path of least resistance to determining what life owes you and what you should expect. Everyone does it. Subconsciously or not, everyone looks around and says, "What do other people like me have? What do they do? Because that's what I should have and do as well."

And this, I think, is a window into understanding why we yearn for the 1950s, despite today being better by almost any measure.

———————

Money buys happiness in the same way drugs bring pleasure: incredible if done right, dangerous if used to mask a weakness, and disastrous when no amount is enough.

What was so unique about the 1950s was the ability for people to find financial balance in a way that before and since has felt elusive.

World War II left its mark on America economically and socially. Between 1942 and 1945, virtually all wages were set by the National War Labor Board, which favored flatter pay—a smaller gap between low-income and high-income workers—than would otherwise exist.

Part of that philosophy stuck around even after wage controls were lifted. The variance of income between classes that existed before the war shrank dramatically. A few years after the war, historian Frederick Lewis Allen noted that the biggest economic gains in percentage terms had gone to the lowest-earning members of society, considerably closing the gap between rich and poor.

If you look at the 1950s and ask, "What was different that

made it feel so great?" this is at least part of your answer. The gap between you and most of the people around you wasn't that large.

It created an era when it was easy to keep your expectations in check because few people in your social circle lived dramatically better than you did.

Many (but not all) Americans could look around and find that not only were they living comfortable lives, they were living lives that were just about as comfortable as those around them whom they compared themselves to.

It's the one thing that distinguiishes the 1950s from other eras.

So the comparatively lower wages than those of today felt great because everyone else earned a lower wage too.

The smaller homes felt nice because everyone else lived in smaller homes too.

The lack of health care was acceptable because your neighbors were in the same circumstances.

Hand-me-downs were acceptable clothes because everyone else wore them.

Camping was an adequate vacation because that's what everyone else did.

It was the one modern era when there wasn't much social pressure to increase your expectations beyond your income. Economic growth accrued straight to happiness. People weren't just better off; they *felt* better off.

And it was short-lived, of course.

By the early 1980s, the postwar togetherness that dominated the 1950s and '60s gave way to more stratified growth, where many people plodded along while a few grew exponentially wealthier. The glorious lifestyles of the few inflated the aspirations of the many.

Rockefeller never yearned for Advil because he didn't know it existed. But social media today adds a new element, in which everyone in the world can see the lifestyles—often inflated, faked, and airbrushed—of other people. You compare yourself to your peers through a curated highlight reel of their lives, where positives are embellished and negatives are hidden from view. Psychologist Jonathan Haidt says people don't really communicate on social media so much as they perform for one another. You see the cars other people drive, the homes they live in, the expensive schools they go to. The ability to say, *I want that, why don't I have that? Why does he get it but I don't?* is so much greater now than it was just a few generations ago.

Today's economy is good at generating three things: wealth, the ability to show off wealth, and great envy for other people's wealth.

It's become so much easier in recent decades to look around and say, "I may have more than I used to. But relative to that person over there, I don't feel like I'm doing that great."

Part of that envy is useful, because saying "I want what they have" is such a powerful motivator of progress.

Yet the point stands: We might have higher incomes, more wealth, and bigger homes—but it's all so quickly smothered by inflated expectations.

This isn't to say the 1950s were better, or fairer, or even that we should strive to rebuild the old system—that's a different topic.

But nostalgia for the 1950s is one of the best examples of what happens when expectations grow faster than circumstances.

In many ways it's always been like that and always will be. Being driven by what other people have and you don't is an unavoidable trait in most people.

It also highlights just how important managing expectations can be if you want to live a happy life.

There are so many examples of this that defy intuition.

Actor Will Smith wrote in his biography that:

- Becoming famous is amazing.
- Being famous is a mixed bag.
- Losing fame is miserable.

The amount of fame almost doesn't matter. Going from a nobody to a little famous creates a huge gap between what you expected your life to be and what it became—same on the way down, in the other direction. But being famous merely meets expectations.

Tennis player Naomi Osaka said that she got to a point in her career when winning a tournament didn't bring her any joy—"I feel more like a relief," she said.

Harry Truman—a failed retailer, failed farmer, failed zinc miner, failed oil driller, and senator held on a leash by local Missouri businessmen—was almost universally panned when he became president after Franklin Roosevelt died. *The Washington Post* wrote: "We should be less than candid at this grave moment if we did not recognize the great disparity between Mr. Truman's experience and the responsibilities that have been thrust upon him." David McCullough wrote: "To many it was not just that the greatest of men had fallen, but that the least of men—or at any rate the least likely of men—had assumed his place." Today, Truman is consistently ranked among historians' top ten presidents of all time, often ahead of Roosevelt.

Part of the reason, I've come to believe, is that expectations for Truman's abilities were so low that any leadership qualities he exhibited blew people's minds. A little success was a win; a big success felt like a miracle.

Actual circumstances don't make much difference in all these cases. What generates the emotion is the big gap between expectations and reality.

When you think of it like that, you realize how powerful expectations are. They can make a celebrity feel miserable and a destitute family feel amazing. It's astounding. Everyone, everywhere, doing almost any task, is just in pursuit of some space between expectations and reality.

But that's so easy to overlook.

Peter Kaufman, CEO of Glenair and one of the smartest people you will ever come across, once wrote:

> We tend to take every precaution to safeguard our material possessions because we know what they cost. But at the same time we neglect things which are much more precious because they don't come with price tags attached: The real value of things like our eyesight or relationships or freedom can be hidden to us, because money is not changing hands.

Same with expectations—they're easy to ignore because their value isn't on a price tag.

But your happiness completely relies on expectations.

Your boss's impression of your career relies on them.

Consumer confidence relies on them.

What moves the stock market relies on them.

So why do we pay so little attention to them?

We spend so much effort trying to improve our income, skills, and ability to forecast the future—all good stuff worthy of our attention. But on the other side there's an almost complete ignorance of expectations, especially managing them with as much effort as we put into changing our circumstances.

Imagine a life where almost everything gets better but you never appreciate it because your expectations rise as fast as your circumstances. It's terrifying, and almost as bad as a world where nothing gets better.

When asked, "You seem extremely happy and content. What's your secret to living a happy life?" ninety-eight-year-old Charlie Munger replied:

The first rule of a happy life is low expectations. If you have unrealistic expectations you're going to be miserable your whole life. You want to have reasonable expectations and take life's results, good and bad, as they happen with a certain amount of stoicism.

My friend Brent has a related theory about marriage: It only works when both people want to help their spouse while expecting nothing in return. If you both do that, you're both pleasantly surprised.

These pieces of advice are easier said than done. I think it's often hard to distinguish high expectations from motivation. And low expectations feels like giving up and minimizing your potential.

The only way around that might be recognizing two things.

One is the constant reminder that wealth and happiness is a two-part equation: what you have and what you expect/need. When you realize that each part is equally important, you see that the overwhelming attention we pay to getting more and the negligible attention we put on managing expectations makes little sense, especially because the expectations side can be so much more in your control.

The other is to understand how the expectation game is played. It's a mental game, and it's often crazy and agonizing, but it's a game that everyone is forced to play, so you should be aware of the rules and strategies. It goes like this: You think you want progress, both for yourself and for the world. But most of the time that's not actually what you want. You want to feel a gap between what you expected and what actually happened. And the expectation side of that equation is not only important, but it's often more in your control than managing your circumstances.

Now let's discuss one of the most complex topics in the world: people's minds.

Wild Minds

**People who think about the world
in unique ways you like also think
about the world in unique ways
you won't like.**

ELIUD KIPCHOGE, THE world's best marathon runner, was being held in a staging room during the 2021 Olympic Games in Tokyo. He and two other runners—Bashir Abdi from Belgium and Abdi Nageeye of the Netherlands—were waiting to receive their Olympic medals after the marathon race, which Kipchoge won for the second time.

Logistics of the awards ceremony meant the runners would have to wait for several hours in a cramped, dull room with nothing to do but sit. Abdi and Nageeye later explained that they did what anyone else would do—they pulled out their cell phones, found a Wi-Fi network, and aimlessly scrolled social media.

Kipchoge didn't.

Abdi and Nageeye said he just sat there, staring at the wall, in perfect silence and contentment.

For hours.

"He is not human," Abdi joked.

He is not human.

He doesn't think, act, or behave like an ordinary person.

Some variation of that phrase can be used for most of your role models. You like them because they do things other people would never consider or can't even comprehend.

Some of those traits are awesome, and you should look up to them, maybe even try to emulate.

Others aren't. *Many* aren't.

Something that's built into the human condition is that people who think about the world in unique ways you like almost certainly also think about the world in unique ways you won't like.

It's so easy to overlook, and it causes us to have poor judgment about who we should look up to and what we should expect from very successful people.

The key thing is that unique minds have to be accepted as a full package, because the things they do well and that we admire cannot be separated from the things we wouldn't want for ourselves or we look down upon.

Let me tell you a quick story about a fighter pilot whom everyone needed but no one could stand.

––––––––––

John Boyd was probably the greatest fighter pilot to ever live.

He revolutionized his field more than anyone before or since. A manual he wrote, *Aerial Attack Study*, incorporated as much math into the science of fighting maneuvers as engineers used in building the planes.

His insights were simple but powerful. In one, Boyd realized there was a tactical advantage not in how fast or high a plane could fly, but how quickly it could change course and begin climbing—a discovery that altered not only how pilots thought but how planes were built. He was as close to a flying savant as they come. Boyd's manual, written in his twenties, became the official tactics guide of fighter pilots. It's still used today.

Boyd is known as one of the most influential thinkers in military history. Yet *The New York Times* once described him as "a virtual nonperson . . . even in the Air Force."

That's because as smart as Boyd was, he was a maniac.

He was rude. Erratic. Disobedient. Impatient. He screamed at his superiors to the astonishment of peers, and was once nearly court-martialed for setting ablaze hangars that didn't have proper heating. In meetings he would chew calluses off his hands and spit the dead skin across the table.

The Air Force loved, and needed, Boyd's insights. But they couldn't stand Boyd the man.

Boyd's defining trait was that he thought about flying planes through a totally different lens than other pilots. Like he was using a different part of his brain and playing a different game than everyone else.

That same personality made him naturally indifferent to established customs. So his superiors would, in the same performance report, rave of his contributions but then attempt to block his promotions.

One review said, "This brilliant young officer is an original thinker," but went on, "He is an intense and impatient man who does not respond well to close supervision. He is extremely intolerant of those who attempt to impede his program." While Boyd was writing the definitive book on fighter maneuvers, two colonels denied his promotion.

Boyd was eventually promoted. He was too talented not to be. But throughout his career, no one knew what to do with him. He pissed off a lot of people. He was unique in every way—good, bad, awful, and occasionally illegal.

———————

John Maynard Keynes once purchased a trove of Isaac Newton's original papers at auction.

Many had never been seen before, as they had been stashed away at Cambridge for centuries.

Newton is probably the smartest human to ever live. But Keynes was astonished to find that much of the work was devoted to alchemy, sorcery, and trying to find a potion for eternal life.

Keynes wrote:

> I have glanced through a great quantity of this at least 100,000 words, I should say. It is utterly impossible to deny that it is wholly magical and wholly devoid of scientific value; and also impossible not to admit that Newton devoted years of work to it.

I wonder: Was Newton a genius in spite of being addicted to magic, or was being curious about things that seemed impossible part of what made him so successful?

I think it's impossible to know. But the idea that crazy geniuses sometimes just look *straight-up* crazy is nearly unavoidable.

There's a scene in the movie *Patton* in which the actor portraying the legendary World War II general George Patton meets his Russian counterpart after the war. Speaking through an interpreter, the Russian general proposes a toast.

"My compliments to the general," Patton says, "but please inform him that I do not care to drink with him or any other Russian son of a bitch."

The interpreter is stunned, and says she can't relay that message. Patton insists.

The Russian general responds through the interpreter that he thinks Patton is also a son of a bitch.

Patton laughs hysterically, raises his glass, and says, "Now that's something I can drink to. From one son of a bitch to another!"

That may perfectly sum up how extremely successful people

operate. Of course they have abnormal characteristics. That's why they're successful! And there is no world in which we should assume that all those abnormal characteristics are positive, polite, endearing, or appealing.

Something I've long thought true, and which shows up constantly when you look for it, is that people who are abnormally good at one thing tend to be abnormally bad at something else. It's as if the brain has capacity for only so much knowledge and emotion, and an abnormal skill robs bandwidth from other parts of someone's personality.

Take Elon Musk.

What kind of thirty-two-year-old thinks they can take on GM, Ford, and NASA at the same time? *An utter maniac.* The kind of person who thinks normal constraints don't apply to them—not in an egotistical way, but in a genuine, believe-it-in-your-bones way. Which is also the kind of person who doesn't worry about, say, Twitter etiquette.

A mindset that can dump a personal fortune into colonizing Mars is not the kind of mindset that worries about the downsides of hyperbole. And the kind of person who proposes making Mars habitable by constantly dropping nuclear bombs in its atmosphere is not the kind of person worried about overstepping the boundaries of reality.

The kind of person who says there's a 99.9999 percent chance humanity is a computer simulation is not the kind of person worried about making untenable promises to shareholders.

The kind of person who promises to solve the water problems in Flint, Michigan, within days of trying to save a Thai children's soccer team stuck in a cave, within days of rebuilding the Tesla Model 3 assembly line in a tent, is not the kind of person who views his lawyers signing off as a critical step.

People love the visionary genius side of Musk, but want it to come without the side that operates in his distorted I-don't-care-about-your-customs version of reality. But I don't think those two things can be separated. They're the risk-reward trade-offs of the same personality trait.

Same for John Boyd.

Same for Steve Jobs, who was both a genius and could be a monster of a boss.

Same for Walt Disney, whose ambitions pushed every company he touched to the razor's edge of bankruptcy.

Former U.S. national security advisor McGeorge Bundy once told President John F. Kennedy that trying to go to the moon was a crazy goal. Kennedy responded: "You don't run for president in your forties unless you have a certain moxie."

———————

Part of this idea is realizing that people who are capable of achieving incredible things often take risks that can backfire just as powerfully.

What kind of person makes their way to the top of a successful company, or a big country?

Someone who is determined, optimistic, doesn't take no for an answer, and is relentlessly confident in their own abilities.

What kind of person is likely to go overboard, bite off more than they can chew, and discount risks that are blindingly obvious to others?

Someone who is determined, optimistic, doesn't take no for an answer, and is relentlessly confident in their own abilities.

Reversion to the mean is one of the most common stories in history. It's the main character in economies, markets, countries, companies, careers—everything. Part of the reason it happens is because the same personality traits that push people to the top also increase the odds of pushing them over the edge.

This is true for countries, particularly empires. A country determined to expand by acquiring more land is unlikely to be run by a person capable of saying, "Okay, that's enough. Let's be thankful for what we have and stop invading other countries." They'll keep pushing until they meet their match. Novelist Stefan Zweig said, "History reveals no instances of a conqueror being surfeited by conquests," meaning no conqueror gets what they wish and then retires.

Perhaps the most important part of this topic is gaining better insight into who we should look up to, particularly who we want to be and who we want to emulate. Naval Ravikant once wrote:

> One day, I realized with all these people I was jealous of, I couldn't just choose little aspects of their life. I couldn't say I want his body, I want her money, I want his personality. You have to be that person. Do you want to actually be that person with all of their reactions, their desires, their family, their happiness level, their outlook on life, their self-image? If you're not willing to do a wholesale, 24/7, 100 percent swap with who that person is, then there is no point in being jealous.

Either you want someone else's life or you don't. Either is equally powerful. Just know which is which when finding role models.

———————

"You gotta challenge all assumptions. If you don't, what is doctrine on day one becomes dogma forever after," John Boyd once said.

That's the kind of philosophy you'll always be remembered for—for better or worse.

Next up: let's talk a little about how bad people are at math.

Wild Numbers

People don't want accuracy.
They want certainty.

The fundamental cause of the trouble is that in the modern world
the stupid are cocksure while the intelligent are full of doubt.

—*Bertrand Russell*

JERRY SEINFELD WAS once driving around in his car with
Jimmy Fallon.

It was an old car, built in the 1950s.

"Do you worry that the car doesn't have an airbag?" Fallon asked.

"No. And be honest," Seinfeld said, "in your whole life how
often have you needed an airbag?"

It was a joke. But what a perfect example of how hard it is for
people to think about probability and uncertainty.

To help his students think about this, Stanford professor
Ronald Howard asked them to write a percentage representing
the likelihood that they had responded correctly next to each
answer on the tests he gave.

If you said you were 100 percent confident that your answer was correct and it turned out to be wrong, you failed the entire test.

If you said you were zero percent confident and your answer happened to be correct, you got no credit.

Everything in between gave you a confidence-adjusted score.

I've never heard of a better way to teach people that life is about managing probabilities. And what an amazing way to scare the daylights out of students, forcing them to realize the consequences of assuming that certainty exists in a world filled with unknowns.

A common trait of human behavior is the burning desire for certainty despite living in an uncertain and probabilistic world.

Dealing with the math behind risk and uncertainty in general is difficult—something people have struggled with forever and always will. That something can be likely and not happen, or unlikely and still happen, is one of the world's most important tricks.

There's a scene in the movie *Zero Dark Thirty* in which the CIA director questions a group of analysts who claim to have located Osama bin Laden.

"I'm about to go look the president in the eye," he says. "And what I'd like to know, no bullshit, very simply, is he there, or is he not there?"

The team's leader says there's a 60 percent to 80 percent chance Bin Laden is in the compound.

"Is that a yes or a no?" the director asks.

Most people get that certainty is rare, and the best you can do is make decisions in which the odds are in your favor. They understand you can be smart and end up wrong, or dumb and end up right, because that's how luck and risk work.

But few people actually use probability in the real world, especially when judging others' success.

Most of what people care about is, "Were you right or wrong?" "Was that a yes or a no?"

Probability is about nuance and gradation. But in the real world people pay attention to black-and-white results.

If you said something will happen and it happens, you were right. If you said it will happen and it doesn't, you were wrong. That's how people think, because it requires the least amount of effort. It's hard to convince others—or yourself—that there could have been an alternative outcome when there's a real-world outcome sitting in front of you.

The core here is that people think they want an accurate view of the future, but what they really crave is certainty.

It's normal to want to rid yourself of the painful reality of not knowing what's going to happen next. Someone who tells you there's a 60 percent chance of a recession happening doesn't do much to ease that pain. They might be adding to it. But someone who says "There is going to be a recession this year" offers something to grab on to with both hands, something that feels like taking control of your future.

After the bin Laden raid, President Obama said the odds placed on whether the terrorist leader was actually in the target house were fifty-fifty. A few years ago I heard one of the SEALs involved in the mission speak at a conference. He said that regardless of whether bin Laden was in the house, the team felt the odds they'd all be killed in the mission were also fifty-fifty. So here we have very high odds that the raid would have ended in disappointment or catastrophe.

It didn't—but the alternative outcome isn't a world many pay much attention to.

We rarely do.

Probability and uncertainty are just so difficult for us to comprehend.

A related and equally important problem here is how easy it is to underestimate rare events in a world as large as ours.

Daniel Kahneman once said, "Human beings cannot comprehend very large or very small numbers. It would be useful for us to acknowledge that fact."

Evelyn Marie Adams won $3.9 million in the New Jersey lottery in 1986. Four months later she won again, collecting another $1.4 million.

"I'm going to quit playing," she told *The New York Times*. "I'm going to give everyone else a chance."

It was a big story at the time, because number crunchers put the odds of her double win at a staggering 1 in 17 trillion.

Three years later two mathematicians, Persi Diaconis and Frederick Mosteller, threw cold water on the excitement.

If one person plays the lottery, the odds of picking the winning numbers twice are indeed 1 in 17 trillion.

But if 100 million people play the lottery week after week—which is the case in America—the odds that *someone* will win twice are actually quite good. Diaconis and Mosteller figured it was 1 in 30.

That number didn't make many headlines.

"With a large enough sample, any outrageous thing is apt to happen," Mosteller said.

That's part of why the world seems so crazy, and why once-in-a-lifetime events seem to happen regularly.

There are about eight billion people on this planet. So if an event has a one-in-a-million chance of occurring every day, it should happen to eight thousand people a day, or 2.9 million times a year, and maybe a quarter of a billion times during your lifetime. Even a one-in-a-billion event will become the fate of hundreds of thousands of people during your lifetime. And given the news media's insatiable appetite for shocking headlines, the odds are nearly 100 percent that you will hear about these events when they happen.

Physicist Freeman Dyson once explained that what's often attributed to the supernatural, or magic, or miracles, is actually just basic math.

> In any normal person's life, miracles should occur at the rate of roughly one per month: The proof of the law is simple. During the time that we are awake and actively engaged in living our lives, roughly for eight hours each day, we see and hear things happening at a rate of one per second. So the total number of events that happen to us is about 30,000 per day, or about a million per month.

If the chance of a "miracle" is one in a million, we should therefore experience one per month, on average.

The idea that incredible things happen because of boring statistics is important, because it's true for terrible things too.

Think about one-hundred-year events. One-hundred-year floods, hurricanes, earthquakes, financial crises, frauds, pandemics, political meltdowns, economic recessions, and so on endlessly. Lots of terrible things can be called one-hundred-year events.

A one-hundred-year event doesn't mean it happens every one hundred years. It means there's about a 1 percent chance of it occurring in any given year. That seems low. But when there are hundreds of different independent one-hundred-year events, what are the odds that one of them will occur in a given year?

Pretty good.

If next year there's a 1 percent chance of a new disastrous pandemic, a 1 percent chance of a crippling depression, a 1 percent chance of a catastrophic flood, a 1 percent chance of political collapse, and on and on, then the odds that *something* bad will happen next year—or any year—are . . . not bad.

It's always been like that. Even periods that we remember as stretches of good times were pockmarked with chaos. The glorious 1950s were actually a continuous chain of grief: Adjusted for population growth, more Americans lost their jobs during the 1958 recession than did in any single month during the Great Recession of 2008. Same with the 1990s: We remember it as a calm decade, but the global financial system nearly fell apart in 1998, during the greatest prosperity boom we've ever seen.

What's different now is the size of the global economy, which increases the sample size of potential crazy things that might happen. When eight billion people interact, the odds of a fraudster, a genius, a terrorist, an idiot, a savant, a jerk, or a visionary moving the needle in a significant way on any given day is nearly guaranteed.

There have been roughly 100 billion humans to ever live. With an average age of roughly thirty years, individual humans have lived something like 1.2 quadrillion days (or 1.2 million billion). Crazy things that have a one-in-a-billion chance of happening have occurred millions of times.

But the problem is far worse now than it's ever been, and will almost certainly continue getting worse.

Frederick Lewis Allen describes how Americans stayed informed in the year 1900:

> It is hard for us today to realize how very widely communities were separated from one another. . . . To some extent a Maine fisherman, an Ohio farmer, and a Chicago businessman would be able to discuss politics with one another, but in the absence of syndicated newspaper columns appearing from coast to coast their information would be based mostly upon what they had read in very divergent local newspapers.

Information was harder to disseminate over distances, and what was going on in other parts of the country or the world just wasn't your top concern; information was local because life was local.

Radio changed that in a big way. It connected people to a common source of information.

TV did it even more.

The internet took it to the next level.

Social media blew it up by orders of magnitude.

Digital news has by and large killed local newspapers and made information global. Eighteen hundred U.S. print media outlets disappeared between 2004 and 2017.

The decline of local news has all kinds of implications. One that doesn't get much attention is that the wider the news becomes the more likely it is to be pessimistic.

Two things make that so:

- Bad news gets more attention than good news because pessimism is seductive and feels more urgent than optimism.
- The odds of a bad news story—a fraud, a corruption, a disaster—occurring in your local town at any given moment is low. When you expand your attention nationally, the odds increase. When they expand globally, the odds of something terrible happening in any given moment are 100 percent.

To exaggerate only a little: Local news reports on softball tournaments. Global news reports on plane crashes and genocides.

A researcher once ranked the sentiment of news over time and found that media outlets all over the world have become steadily more gloomy over the last sixty years.

Compare this to the past. Here's Frederick Lewis Allen again, writing about life in 1900:

The majority of Americans were less likely than their descendants to be dogged by that frightening sense of insecurity which comes from being jostled by forces—economic, political, international—beyond one's personal ken. Their horizons were close to them.

Their horizons were close to them. In modern times our horizons cover every nation, culture, political regime, and economy in the world.

There are so many good things that come from that.

But we shouldn't be surprised that the world feels historically broken in recent years and will continue that way going forward. It's not—we just see more of the bad stuff that's always happened than we ever saw before.

The world breaks about once every ten years, on average—always has, always will. Sometimes it feels like terrible luck, or that bad news has new momentum. More often it's just raw math at work. A zillion different things can go wrong, so at least one of them is likely to be causing havoc at any given moment. And given how connected we are, you're going to hear about it.

A few things to keep in mind here.

People don't want accuracy. They want certainty.

A lot of what goes on in the prediction world is an attempt to rid yourself of the painful reality of not knowing what's going to happen next. When you realize that making people feel better is more appealing than giving people useful figures, you start to see why thinking in probabilities is rare.

Charlie Munger gave a talk in the 1990s called "The Psychology of Human Misjudgment." He listed twenty-five biases that lead to bad decisions. One is the "Doubt-Avoidance Tendency," which he described:

The brain of man is programmed with a tendency to quickly remove doubt by reaching some decision.

It is easy to see how evolution would make animals, over the eons, drift toward such quick elimination of doubt. After all, the one thing that is surely counterproductive for a prey animal that is threatened by a predator is to take a long time in deciding what to do.

Professor Philip Tetlock has spent most of his career studying experts, self-proclaimed or otherwise. A big takeaway from his research is how awful so many experts are at predicting politics and the economy. Given that track record, will people ever choose to ignore the experts? "No way," Tetlock once said. "We need to believe we live in a predictable, controllable world, so we turn to authoritative-sounding people who promise to satisfy that need."

The inability to forecast the past has no impact on our desire to forecast the future. Certainty is so valuable that we'll never give up the quest for it, and most people couldn't get out of bed in the morning if they were honest about how uncertain the future is.

It often takes too long for a sufficient sample size to play out. So everyone is left guessing.

Let's say you're a seventy-five-year-old economist. You started your career at age twenty-five. So you have half a century of experience predicting what the economy will do next. You're as seasoned as they come.

But how many recessions have there been in the last fifty years? Seven.

There have only been seven times in your career that you've been able to measure your skills.

If you want to really judge someone's abilities you would

compare dozens, hundreds, or thousands of attempts against reality. But a lot of fields don't generate that many opportunities to measure. It's no one's fault; it's just that the reality of the real world is messier than an idealized spreadsheet.

It's an important quirk, because if someone says there's an 80 percent chance of a recession, the only way to tell if they're right is to compare dozens or hundreds of times they made that exact call and see if it came true 80 percent of the time.

If you don't have dozens or hundreds of attempts—sometimes you only have one or two—there's no way to know whether someone who says 75 percent chance of this or 32 percent chance of that is right or not. So we're all left guessing (or preferring those who profess certainty).

Distinguishing between unfortunate odds and recklessness is hard when risk has painful consequences. It's easier to see black and white even when the odds are apparent.

I valeted at a hotel in college. Our team parked ten thousand cars a month. And we banged one of them up every month, like clockwork.

Management found this intolerable. Every few weeks we'd be scolded for our recklessness.

But one accident in ten thousand parks is pretty good. If you drive twice a day, it'll take you fourteen years to park ten thousand times. One bent fender every fourteen years is a driving record your insurance company won't bat an eye at.

But try explaining that to your boss, who had to file so many damage reports they got to know the insurance claims adjusters by name. You'll get no sympathy. It's so much easier to say, "You guys are clearly being reckless. Slow down or you're fired."

The same thing happens in many parts of life. Take the stock market. You can show people that the market historically crashes every five to seven years. But every five to seven years people say, "This is wrong, this feels broken, my advisor screwed up." Knowing the high odds of something happening loses its meaning when that thing happening hurts. Probability goes out the window.

What you always want to avoid are catastrophic risks. A pilot who crashes once every ten thousand flights is a catastrophe. But our difficulty dealing with probability and large numbers makes us overly sensitive to run-of-the-mill, inevitable risks.

Same as ever.

In the next chapter, we'll look at a little-known fact about Martin Luther King Jr.'s most famous speech and at the incredible power of stories.

Best Story
Wins

Stories are always more powerful
than statistics.

THE BEST STORY wins.

Not the best idea, or the right idea, or the most rational idea. Just whoever tells a story that catches people's attention and gets them to nod their heads is the one who tends to be rewarded.

Great ideas explained poorly can go nowhere, while old or wrong ideas told compellingly can ignite a revolution. Morgan Freeman can narrate a grocery list and bring people to tears, while an inarticulate scientist might cure a disease and go unnoticed.

There is too much information in the world for everyone to calmly sift through the data, looking for the most rational, most correct answer. People are busy and emotional, and a good story is always more powerful and persuasive than ice-cold statistics.

If you have the right answer, you may or may not get ahead.

If you have the wrong answer but you're a good storyteller, you'll probably get ahead (for a while).

If you have the right answer and you're a good storyteller, you'll almost certainly get ahead.

That's always been true, always will be true, and it shows up in so many areas of history.

Martin Luther King Jr.'s famous speech at the Lincoln Memorial on August 28, 1963, did not go according to plan.

King's advisor and speechwriter, Clarence Jones, drafted a full speech for King to deliver, based on, he recalled, a "summary of ideas we had talked about."

The first few minutes of King's speech followed the script. Video shows him constantly looking down at his notes, reading verbatim. "Go back to Georgia, go back to Louisiana, go back to the slums and ghettos of our northern cities, knowing that somehow this situation can and will be changed."

Just then, around halfway through the speech, gospel singer Mahalia Jackson—who was standing to King's left, maybe ten feet away—shouts out, "Tell 'em about the dream, Martin! Tell 'em about the dream!"

Jones recalled: "[King] looks over at her in real time, then he takes the text of the written speech and he slides it to the left side of the lectern. He grabs the lectern and looks out on more than 250,000 people."

There's then a six-second pause before King looks up at the sky and says:

> I have a dream. It is a dream deeply rooted in the American dream.

I have a dream that one day this nation will rise up and live out the true meaning of its creed: "We hold these truths to be self-evident, that all men are created equal."

I have a dream that my four little children will one day live in a nation where they will not be judged by the color of their skin but by the content of their character.

I have a dream today!

The rest was history.

Jones said, "That portion of the speech which is most celebrated in this country and around the world is not the speech that he planned to give."

It wasn't what King prepared. It wasn't what he and his speechwriter assumed would be the best material for that day.

But it was one of the best stories ever told, evoking emotion and connecting the dots in millions of people's heads in a way that changed history.

Good stories tend to do that. They have extraordinary ability to inspire and evoke positive emotions, bringing insight and attention to topics that people tend to ignore when they've previously been presented with nothing but facts.

Mark Twain was perhaps the best storyteller of modern times. When editing his writing, he would read aloud to his wife and kids. When a passage caused them to look bored, he would cut it. When their eyes widened, when they sat forward or furrowed their brow, he knew he was onto something, and he doubled down.

Even within a good story, a powerful phrase or sentence can do most of the work. There is a saying that people don't remember books; they remember sentences.

C. R. Hallpike is an anthropologist who once wrote a review of a young author's new book on the history of humans. The review states:

It would be fair to say that whenever his facts are broadly correct they are not new, and whenever he tries to strike out on his own he often gets things wrong, sometimes seriously. . . . [It is not] a contribution to knowledge.

Two things are notable here.

One is that the author, Yuval Noah Harari, has sold over twenty-eight million books, making him one of the bestselling contemporary authors in any field, and his book *Sapiens*—which Hallpike was reviewing—is the most successful anthropology book of all time.

The other is that Harari doesn't seem to disagree with Hallpike's assessment.

Harari once said about writing *Sapiens*:

I thought, "This is so banal!" . . . There is absolutely nothing there that is new. I'm not an archeologist. I'm not a primatologist. I mean, I did *zero* new research. . . . It was really reading the kind of common knowledge and just presenting it in a new way.

What *Sapiens* does have is excellent writing. *Beautiful* writing. The stories are captivating, the flow is effortless. Harari took what was already known and wrote it better than anyone had done before. The result was fame greater than anyone before him could imagine. Best story wins.

It's nothing to be ashamed of, because so many successes work this way.

The Civil War is probably the most well-documented period in American history. There are thousands of books analyzing every conceivable angle, chronicling every possible detail. But in 1990 Ken Burns's *The Civil War* documentary became an instant phenomenon, with forty million viewers and winning forty major television and film awards. As many Americans watched Ken Burns's *Civil War* in 1990 as watched the Super Bowl that year.

And all Burns did—not to minimize it, because it's such a feat—is take 130-year-old existing information and weave it into a (very) good story.

Burns once described perhaps the most important part of his storytelling process—the music that accompanies images in his documentaries:

> I went into old hymnals and old song books and I had someone plunk them out on the piano. And whenever something hit me I'd go, "That one!" And then we'd go into a studio with a session musician and probably do thirty different recordings.

Burns says that when writing a documentary script he will literally extend a sentence so that it lines up with a certain beat in the background music; he will cut a sentence to do the same. "Music is God," he says. "It's not just the icing on the cake. It's the fudge, baked right in there."

Now imagine you're a world-class historian who has spent decades uncovering new and groundbreaking information about an important topic. How much time do you spend thinking about whether a specific sentence of what you've discovered will match the beat of a song? Probably none. Ken Burns does. And that is why he's a household name.

Author Bill Bryson is the same. His books fly off the shelves, which can drive the little-known academics who uncovered the things he writes about crazy. One of his books—*The Body: A Guide for Occupants*—is basically an anatomy textbook. It has no new information, no discoveries. But it's so well written—he tells such a good story—that it became an instant *New York Times* bestseller and *The Washington Post*'s Book of the Year.

There are so many examples of this.

Charles Darwin was not the first to discover evolution; he just wrote the first and most compelling book about it.

Professor John Burr Williams had more profound insight on the topic of valuing stocks than Benjamin Graham. But Graham knew how to write a good paragraph, so he became the legend and sold millions of books.

Andrew Carnegie said he was as proud of his charm and ability to befriend people as he was of his business acumen. Elon Musk is as skilled at getting investors to believe a vision as he is at engineering.

Everyone knows the story of the sinking of the *Titanic*, which claimed fifteen hundred lives.

But almost no one ever mentions a word about the 1948 sinking of the Chinese ferryboat SS *Kiangya*, which claimed nearly four thousand lives.

Or the 1987 sinking of the ferryboat MV *Dona Paz*, which killed 4,345 people.

Or the capsizing of the MV *Le Joola*, which claimed 1,863 lives off the coast of Gambia in 2002.

Perhaps the *Titanic* sticks out because of its story potential: the famous and wealthy passengers, the firsthand accounts from survivors, and, of course, the eventual blockbuster movie.

The influence of a good story drives you crazy if you assume the world is swayed by facts and objectivity—if you assume the best idea or the largest numbers or the correct answer wins. There's a devoted group of Harari critics obsessed with showing how unoriginal his work is; Musk is viewed with the same mix of confusion and contempt.

In a perfect world, the importance of information wouldn't rely on its author's eloquence. But we live in a world where people are bored, impatient, emotional, and need complicated things distilled into easy-to-grasp scenes.

If you look, I think you'll find that wherever information is exchanged—wherever there are products, companies, careers, politics, knowledge, education, and culture—the best story wins.

Stephen Hawking once noted of his bestselling physics books: "Someone told me that each equation I included in the book would halve the sales." Readers don't want a lecture; they want a memorable story.

Winston Churchill was, by most accounts, a mediocre politician. But he was a master storyteller and orator, a savant at getting people's attention through motivation and provoking emotion—which is what made all the difference during his time in office.

Or take the stock market. The valuation of every company is simply a number from today multiplied by a story about tomorrow. Some companies are incredibly good at telling stories, and during some eras investors become captivated by the wildest ideas of what the future might bring. If you're trying to figure out where something is going next, you have to understand more than its technical possibilities. You have to understand the stories everyone tells themselves about those possibilities, because it's such a big part of the forecasting equation.

Perhaps no one has mastered the art of storytelling better than comedians. They are the best thought leaders because they understand how the world works, but they want to make you laugh rather than make themselves feel smart. They take insights from psychology, sociology, politics, and every other dry field and squeeze out amazing stories. That's why they can sell out arenas while an academic researcher who discovers a great insight about social behavior can go unnoticed.

Mark Twain said, "Humor is a way to show you're smart without bragging."

A few things about good stories worth remembering:

When a topic is complex, stories are like leverage.

Leverage squeezes the full potential out of something with less effort. Stories leverage ideas in the same way that debt leverages assets.

Trying to explain something like physics is hard if you're deadlifting facts and formulas. But if you can explain things like how fire works with a story about balls rolling down hills and running into one another—that's what physicist Richard Feynman, an astounding storyteller, used to do—you can explain something complex in seconds, without much effort.

Stories do more than persuade others. They can help you just as much. Part of what made Albert Einstein so talented was his imagination and ability to distill complexity into a simple scene in his head. When he was sixteen he started imagining what it would be like to ride on a beam of light, holding on to the sides like a flying carpet and thinking through how it would travel and bend. Soon after, he began imagining what your body would feel like if you were in an enclosed elevator riding through space. He contemplated gravity by imagining bowling balls and billiard balls competing for space on a trampoline surface. He could process a textbook of information with the effort of a daydream.

Ken Burns once said, "The common stories are one plus one equals two. We get it, they make sense. But the good stories are about one plus one equals three." That's leverage.

The most persuasive stories are about what you want to believe is true, or are an extension of what you've experienced firsthand.

Poet Ralph Hodgson put this well when he said, "Some things have to be believed to be seen." Poor evidence can be a very compelling story if that story scratches an itch someone wants to go away, or gives context to a belief they want to be true.

Stories get diverse people to focus attention on a single point.

Steven Spielberg noted this:

> The most amazing thing for me is that every single person who sees a movie . . . brings a whole set of unique experiences. Now, through careful manipulation and good storytelling, you can get everybody to clap at the same time, to laugh at the same time, and to be afraid at the same time.

Mark Twain once said he knew he was a successful author when Kaiser Wilhelm II said he'd read every Twain book, and later that day a porter at his hotel said the same. "Great books are wine," Twain said, "but my books are water. But everybody drinks water." He found the universal emotions that influence everyone, regardless of who they were or where they were from, and got them to nod their heads in the same direction. It's nearly magic.

Guiding people's attention to a single point is one of the most powerful life skills.

**Good stories create so much hidden opportunity
among things you assume can't be improved.**

How many great ideas have already been discovered but could grow one hundred times or more if someone explained them better?

How many products have found only a fraction of their potential market because the companies that made them are so bad at describing them to customers?

So, so many.

Visa founder Dee Hock once said, "New ways of looking at things create much greater innovation than new ways of doing them."

You'll get discouraged if you think every new book has to be about an original idea, or that every new company has to sell a brand-new invention. There is so much more opportunity if you see the world like Yuval Noah Harari—that it's not what you say or what you do, but how you say it and how you present it.

**Some of the most important questions to ask yourself
are: Who has the right answer, but I ignore because
they're inarticulate? And what do I believe is true but
is actually just good marketing?**

They are uncomfortable questions and difficult to answer. But if you're honest with yourself you'll see how many people, and how many beliefs, fall into these buckets. And then you'll see the truth—that the best story wins.

———————

Next I'll share another timeless truth: It has to do with war, fitness, stock markets, and other crazy things that cannot be measured.

Does Not Compute

The world is driven by forces that cannot be measured.

A LOT OF THINGS don't make any sense. The numbers don't add up, the explanations are full of holes. And yet they keep happening—people making crazy decisions and reacting in bizarre ways that seem to defy rational thinking.

Most decisions aren't made on a spreadsheet, where you just add up the numbers and a clear answer pops out. There's a human element that's hard to quantify and explain, and that can seem totally detached from the original goal, yet it carries more influence than anything else.

Historian Will Durant once said, "Logic is an invention of man and may be ignored by the universe." And it often is, which can drive you mad if you expect the world to work in rational ways.

Attempting to distill emotional and hormonal humans into a

math equation is the cause of so much frustration and surprise in the world.

———————

Robert McNamara was hired by Henry Ford II to help turn Ford Motors around. Ford was losing money after World War II and needed a "whiz kid"—that's what Henry Ford called it—who saw running a business as an operations science, driven by the ice-cold truth of statistics.

Later, McNamara took that skill to Washington when he became Secretary of Defense during the Vietnam War. He demanded that everything be quantified, with daily, weekly, and monthly charts tracking the progress of every imaginable wartime statistic.

But the strategy that worked at Ford had a flaw when applied at the Department of Defense. Edward Lansdale, head of special operations at the Pentagon, once looked at McNamara's numbers. He said something was missing.

"What?" McNamara asked.

"The feelings of the Vietnamese people," Lansdale replied.

You couldn't reduce that to a statistic or a chart.

This was a central issue with managing the Vietnam War. The difference between battle statistics brought to Washington and the feelings among those involved could be a million miles apart. General Westmoreland, who commanded U.S. forces, told Senator Fritz Hollings, "We're killing these people at a rate of ten to one." Hollings replied, "The American people don't care about the ten. They care about the one."

Ho Chi Minh once put it more bluntly, allegedly stating: "You will kill ten of us, and we will kill one of you, but it is you who will tire first."

It's hard to contextualize that on a chart.

Some things are immeasurably important. They're either

impossible, or too elusive, to quantify. But they can make all the difference in the world, often because their lack of quantification causes people to discount their relevance or even deny their existence.

Carved on the wall at University of Chicago is a quote from Lord Kelvin that says, "When you cannot measure, your knowledge is meager and unsatisfactory."

He's not wrong, but the danger is assuming that if something can't be measured it doesn't matter. The opposite is true: Some of the most important forces in the world—particularly those regarding people's personalities and mindsets—are nearly impossible to measure and impossible to predict.

Jeff Bezos once said, "The thing I have noticed is when the anecdotes and the data disagree, the anecdotes are usually right. There's something wrong with the way you are measuring it."

I love and hate that quote in equal parts, because I know it's true but I don't want it to be. You see its wisdom so often in history.

The Battle of the Bulge was one of the deadliest American military battles of all time. Nineteen thousand American soldiers were killed, another seventy thousand wounded or missing, in just over a month as Nazi Germany made an ill-fated final push against the Allies.

Part of the reason it was so bloody is that Americans were surprised. And part of the reason they were surprised is that in the rational minds of American generals, it made no sense for Germany to attack.

The Germans didn't have enough troops to mount a successful counterattack, and the few that were left were often children under age eighteen with no combat experience. They didn't have enough fuel. They were running out of food. The terrain of the Ardennes Forest in Belgium stacked the odds against them. The weather was atrocious.

The Allies knew all this. They reasoned that any rational German commander would not launch a counterattack. So the American lines were left fairly thin and ill-supplied.

And then, *boom*. The Germans attacked anyway.

What the American generals overlooked was how unhinged Hitler had become. He wasn't rational. He was living in his own world, detached from reality and reason. When his generals asked where they should get fuel to complete the attack, Hitler said they could steal it from the Americans. Reality didn't matter.

Historian Stephen Ambrose notes that Eisenhower and General Omar Bradley got all the war-planning reasoning and logic right in late 1944, except for one detail—the extent to which Hitler had lost his mind.

An aide to Bradley mentioned during the war: "If we were fighting reasonable people they would have surrendered long ago." But they weren't, and it—the one thing that was hard to measure with logic—mattered more than anything.

Archibald Hill ran every morning, starting on a track at 7:15. He was good at it—a great athlete and competitive runner.

Hill, a British physiologist born in 1886, was in many ways a perfect scientist, because he devoted most of his career to answering a question he was personally interested in and could test on himself: How fast and how far can people run?

Given my body, or your body, or Hill's own body, what's the theoretical limit to how much we can push ourselves? That's the question he wanted to answer.

Hill's early work was based on the idea that maximum running performance is a function of an athlete's muscles—overwhelmingly their heart. If my heart can pump more blood to my running muscles than yours, I can run faster. It was something you could cleanly measure, and Hill won the Nobel

Prize in medicine in 1922 for some of his work in understanding body mechanics.

The idea that you can measure the limit of how fast someone can run made sense, and in the laboratory and on the test track it more or less holds up.

On the racetrack, in the real world, it's a different story. Hill's calculations had almost zero ability to predict race winners.

If the best competitive athletes merely had the strongest hearts and the greatest capacity to transport oxygen, finding and knowing who will be the best athlete would be straightforward.

But it's not.

Great athletes are more likely to have stronger hearts than a couch potato. But the correlation between cardiovascular capacity and athletic performance is far from perfect, which is why competitive races like marathons and Olympic sprints are exciting. Sometimes great athletes choke. Sometimes dark horses win.

Hill, once wedded to the idea that running performance should be tied solely to muscular ability, was stumped. Asked why his initial calculations of athletic ability were of little use at predicting race winners, he responded: "To tell you the truth, we don't do it because it is useful, but because it's amusing."

But he eventually figured out what was going on, and it changed how scientists think about athletic performance forever.

Athletic performance isn't just what you're physically capable of. It's what you're capable of within the context of what your brain is willing to endure for the risk and reward in a given moment.

Your brain's first job is to make sure you don't die. So like a speed governor on a car, it won't let you exert true maximum performance—which could leave you exhausted to the point of being vulnerable—unless the stakes are high enough. It will shut you down at a lower physical "limit" if the risk of exertion isn't worth the reward.

Physical running limits on a test track may be different than physical limits during an Olympic final, which may be different than physical limits when being chased by an ax murderer.

This helps explain crazy stories about people lifting up cars when someone is pinned underneath, their life in jeopardy. Capabilities are a function of in-the-moment circumstances.

In his early days, Hill wrote that "our bodies are machines, whose energy expenditures may be closely measured."

Later on, as his views came around to a more nuanced view of human performance, he noted that "there is more in athletics than sheer chemistry."

There was a behavioral and psychological side that was much harder to measure.

You never know how an athlete can perform until you put them in the heat of the moment, with the pressures, risks, and incentives of real-world conditions that can't be emulated in the laboratory.

Hill, in an interesting coincidence, was married to John Maynard Keynes's sister.

Keynes, the British economist, had discovered in his work that economies are not machines. They have souls, emotions, and feelings. Keynes called them "animal spirits."

Hill discovered the same, but for our bodies. He called them "moral factors." Our bodies are not machines, and we shouldn't expect them to perform as such. They have feelings, emotions, and fears, all of which regulate what we're capable of.

All of which are very hard to measure.

———

Investor Jim Grant once said:

> To suppose that the value of a common stock is determined purely by a corporation's earnings discounted by the relevant interest rates and adjusted for the marginal tax rate is to forget that people have burned witches, gone to war on a whim, risen

to the defense of Joseph Stalin and believed Orson Welles when he told them over the radio that the Martians had landed.

That's always been the case. And it will always be the case.

Every investment price, every market valuation, is just a number from today multiplied by a story about tomorrow.

The numbers are easy to measure, easy to track, easy to formulate. It's getting easier as almost everyone has cheap access to information.

But the stories are often bizarre reflections of people's hopes, dreams, fears, insecurities, and tribal affiliations. And they're getting more bizarre as social media amplifies the most emotionally appealing views.

A few examples of how powerful this can be:

Lehman Brothers was in great shape on September 10, 2008. Its tier 1 capital ratio—a measure of a bank's ability to endure loss—was 11.7 percent. That was higher than the previous quarter. Higher than Goldman Sachs. Higher than Bank of America. It was more capital than Lehman had in 2007, when the banking industry was about as strong as it had ever been.

Seventy-two hours later Lehman was bankrupt.

The only thing that changed during those three days was investors' faith in the company. One day they believed in the company and bought its debt. The next day that belief stopped, and so did its funding.

That faith is the only thing that mattered. But it was the one thing that was hard to quantify, hard to model, hard to predict, and didn't compute in a traditional valuation model.

GameStop was the opposite. It looked like it was on the edge of going out of business in 2020. Then it became a cultural obsession on Reddit, the stock surged, the company raised a ton of money, and at one point in 2021 it was worth $11 billion.

Same thing here: The most important variable was the stories people told themselves. And that was the only thing you couldn't measure and couldn't predict with foresight. That's why the results don't compute.

Whenever something like this happens you see people shocked and angry about how the world has become detached from fundamentals.

But Grant was right: It's always been like this.

The 1920s were giddy. The '30s were pure panic. The world was coming to an end in the '40s. The '50s, '60s, and '70s were boom to bust, over and over. The '80s and '90s were insane. The 2000s have been like a reality TV show.

If you've relied on data and logic alone to make sense of the economy, you'd have been confused for a hundred years straight.

Economist Per Bylund once noted: "The concept of economic value is easy: whatever someone wants has value, regardless of the reason (if any)."

Not utility, not profits—just whether people want it or not, for *any* reason. So much of what happens in the economy is rooted in emotions, which can, at times, be nearly impossible to make sense of.

To me it's obvious that the one thing you can't measure, can't predict, and can't model in a spreadsheet is the most powerful force in all of business and investing—just like it's the most powerful force in the military. Same in politics. Same in careers. Same in relationships. A lot of things don't compute.

The danger, one you see often in investing, is when people become too McNamara-like—so obsessed with data and so confident in their models that they leave no room for error or surprise. No room for things to be crazy, dumb, unexplainable, and to remain that way for a long time. Always asking "Why is this happening?" and expecting there to be a rational answer. Or worse, always mistaking what happened for what you think should have happened.

The ones who thrive long term are those who understand the real world is a never-ending chain of absurdity, confusion, messy relationships, and imperfect people.

Making sense of that world requires admitting a few things.

———————

John Nash is one of the smartest mathematicians to ever live; he won the Nobel Prize. He was also schizophrenic and spent most of his life convinced that aliens were sending him coded messages.

In her book *A Beautiful Mind*, Sylvia Nasar recounts a conversation between Nash and Harvard professor George Mackey:

> "How could you, a mathematician, a man devoted to reason and logical proof . . . how could you believe that extraterrestrials are sending you messages? How could you believe that you are being recruited by aliens from outer space to save the world? How could you . . . ?"
>
> "Because," Nash said slowly in his soft, reasonable southern drawl, "the ideas I had about supernatural beings came to me the same way that my mathematical ideas did. So I took them seriously."

The first step toward accepting that some things don't compute is realizing that the reason we have innovation and advancement is because we are fortunate to have people in this world whose minds work differently from ours.

It would be great if the world worked in predictable, rational ways. But constant uncertainty, misunderstanding, and the inability to know what people will do next is the truth. Author Robert Greene once wrote, "The need for certainty is the greatest disease the mind faces." It's what causes us to overlook that the world is not one big spreadsheet whose outputs can be computed. We'd never get anywhere if everyone viewed the world as a clean set of rational rules to follow.

The next is accepting that what's rational to one person can be crazy to another. Everything would compute if everyone had the same time horizon, goals, ambitions, and risk tolerances. But they don't. Panic-selling stocks after they've declined 5 percent is a terrible idea if you're a long-term investor, and a career imperative if you're a professional trader. There is no world in which every business or investing decision you see other people make will align with your own hopes and dreams of how things should be.

Third is understanding the power of incentives. A financial bubble might seem irrational, but the people who work in industries that are in bubbles—mortgage brokers in 2004 or stockbrokers in 1999—make so much money from them that there's a powerful incentive to keep the music playing. They delude not only their customers but themselves.

Last is the power of stories over statistics. "Housing prices in relation to median incomes are now above their historic average and typically mean revert" is a statistic. "Jim just made $500,000 flipping homes and can now retire early and his wife thinks he's amazing" is a story. And it's way more persuasive in the moment.

It's hard to compute, but it's how the world works.

In the next chapter, we'll look at life's guaranteed ability to swing from one absurdity to the next.

Calm Plants
the Seeds
of Crazy

**Crazy doesn't mean broken.
Crazy is normal;** *beyond the point
of crazy* **is normal.**

THERE IS A very common life cycle of greed and fear. It goes
like this:

First you assume good news is permanent.

Then you become oblivious to bad news.

Then you ignore bad news.

Then you deny bad news.

Then you panic at bad news.

Then you accept bad news.

Then you assume bad news is permanent.

Then you become oblivious to good news.

Then you ignore good news.

Then you deny good news.

Then you accept good news.

Then you assume good news is permanent.

And we're back where we began. The cycle repeats.

Let's dig deeper on why this cycle happens, and why it always will.

––––––––––

The 1960s were a period of scientific optimism. In the previous fifty years the world had gone from horse and buggy to rockets, and from bloodletting to organ transplants.

This caused a push among economists to try to eradicate the scourge of recessions. If we could launch intercontinental ballistic missiles and walk on the moon, surely we could prevent two quarters of negative GDP growth.

Hyman Minsky, who spent most of his career as an economist at Washington University in St. Louis, was fascinated by the boom-and-bust nature of economies. He also thought the idea of eradicating recessions was nonsense, and always would be.

Minsky's seminal theory was called the financial instability hypothesis.

The idea isn't heavy on math and formulas. It describes a psychological process that basically goes like this:

- When an economy is stable, people get optimistic.
- When people get optimistic, they go into debt.
- When they go into debt, the economy becomes unstable.

Minsky's big idea was that *stability is destabilizing*.

A lack of recessions actually plants the seeds of the next recession, which is why we can never get rid of them.

"Over periods of prolonged prosperity, the economy transits from financial relations that make for a stable system to financial relations that make for an unstable system," he wrote.

A growing belief that things will be okay pushes us—like a law of physics—toward something not going okay.

This applies to so many things.

Imagine a world where the stock market never went down. Market stability is all but assured, and stocks only go up.

What would you do?

You would buy as many stocks as you possibly could. You would mortgage your house and buy more. You'd consider selling a kidney and buy more still. That would be the reasonable thing to do!

And in the process, the price of stocks would get bid up. Their valuations would become ever more expensive. They would get so expensive that their future return prospects would decline close to zero.

And at that very moment, the seeds of breakdown would start to sprout.

The higher stock valuations become, the more sensitive markets are to being caught off guard by life's ability to surprise you in ways you never imagined.

Surprise has six common characteristics:

- Incomplete information
- Uncertainty
- Randomness
- Chance
- Unfortunate timing
- Poor incentives

With assets priced high and no room for error, markets would be hanging on by a thread, crushed at the first sniff of anything less than perfection.

The irony is that when markets are guaranteed not to crash—or more realistically, when people think that's the case—they are far more likely to crash.

The mere idea of stability causes a *smart and rational* movement toward bidding asset prices up high enough to cause instability.

Stability is destabilizing.

Or, put another way: Calm plants the seeds of crazy. Always has, always will.

"Everything feels unprecedented when you haven't engaged with history," writer Kelly Hayes once wrote.

It's such an important idea.

Historian Dan Carlin wrote in his book *The End Is Always Near*:

> Pretty much nothing separates us from human beings in earlier eras than how much less disease affects us. . . . If we moderns lived for one year with the sort of death rates our pre-industrial age ancestors perpetually lived with, we'd be in societal shock.

Modern life in general is about as safe as it's ever been. And effectively all the improvement over the last century has come from a decline in infectious disease. In 1900 roughly eight hundred per one hundred thousand Americans died each year from infectious disease. By 2014 that was forty-six per one hundred thousand—a 94 percent decline.

This decline is probably the best thing ever to happen to humanity.

To follow that sentence with "but" is a step too far. It's an entirely good thing.

However, it creates an anomaly.

The decline in deaths from infectious diseases has made the world less equipped to handle them—maybe not medically, but certainly psychologically. What was a tragic but expected part of life a hundred years ago is now a tragic and *inconceivable* part of modern life—which is indeed what made the COVID-19 pandemic so shocking and overwhelming.

Clark Whelton, a former speechwriter for New York City mayor Ed Koch, once wrote:

> For those who grew up in the 1930s and 1940s, there was nothing unusual about finding yourself threatened by contagious disease. Mumps, measles, chicken pox, and German measles swept through entire schools and towns; I had all four. Polio took a heavy annual toll, leaving thousands of people (mostly children) paralyzed or dead. There were no vaccines. Growing up meant running an unavoidable gauntlet of infectious disease.

Compare this to my generation—who benefit from a half dozen vaccines within weeks of birth—and it's like we live in separate worlds. I can't fathom what was normal two generations ago.

My guess is if COVID-19 struck the world in 1920, it would be a single page in the history books about yet another deadly pandemic wedged in between a long list of common tragedies. But since it struck in the comparative calm of 2020, it will leave a mark that reshapes how some people think about viral risk.

The odd thing to ponder is the Hyman Minsky version of this development.

Did a lack of pandemics over the last fifty years make the world more vulnerable to COVID-19? Did the decline of infectious disease death make us underestimate the odds that it could happen in modern times?

Part of what made COVID dangerous is that we got so good at preventing pandemics in the last century that few people before 2020 assumed an infectious disease would ever impact their lives. It was hard to comprehend. So people were utterly unprepared for a pandemic when it arrived. The irony of good times is that they breed complacency and skepticism of warnings.

Epidemiologists had been warning something like COVID could happen for years—but mostly to deaf ears and a public that assumed pandemics were something that happened only in history books and other parts of the world. It's hard to convince someone they're in danger of a risk they assume has been defeated.

"As public health did its job, it became a target" of budget cuts, Lori Freeman, CEO of the National Association of Health Officials, said in 2020.

Calm planted the seeds of crazy. And that happens so often.

A common irony goes like this:

- Paranoia leads to success because it keeps you on your toes.
- But paranoia is stressful, so you abandon it quickly once you achieve success.
- Now you've abandoned what made you successful and you begin to decline—which is even more stressful.

It happens in business, investing, careers, relationships—all over the place.

Carl Jung had a theory called enantiodromia. It's the idea that an excess of something gives rise to its opposite.

Let me give you an example from Mother Nature.

California was hit with an epic drought in the mid-2010s. Then

2017 came, dropping a preposterous amount of moisture. Parts of Lake Tahoe received—I'm not making this up—more than sixty-five feet of snow in a few months. The six-year drought was declared over.

You'd think that would be great. But it backfired in an unexpected way.

Record rain in 2017 led to record vegetation growth that summer. It was called a superbloom, and it caused even desert towns to be covered in green.

A dry 2018 meant all that vegetation died and became dry kindling. That led to some of the biggest wildfires California had ever seen.

So record rain directly led to record fires.

There's a long history of this, verified by looking at tree rings, which inscribe both heavy rainfall and subsequent fire scars. The two go hand in hand. "A wet year reduces fires while increasing vegetation growth, but then the increased vegetation dries out in subsequent dry years, thereby increasing the fire fuel," the National Oceanic and Atmospheric Administration wrote.

That's hardly intuitive, but here again—calm plans the seeds of crazy.

What calm planting the seeds of crazy does is important: It makes us fundamentally underestimate the odds of things going wrong, and the consequences of something going wrong. Things can become the most dangerous when people perceive them to be the safest.

After slapping Chris Rock on stage at the Oscars, Will Smith turned to Denzel Washington for advice. Washington said, "At your highest moment, be careful. That's when the devil comes for you."

A final word about why things have a tendency of getting out of hand. It's that optimism and pessimism always have to overshoot what seems reasonable, because the only way to discover the limits of what's possible is to venture a little way past those limits.

Jerry Seinfeld had the most popular show on TV. Then he quit.

He later said the reason he killed his show while it was thriving was because the only way to know where the top is, is to experience the decline, which he had no interest in doing. Maybe the show could keep rising, maybe it couldn't. He was fine not knowing the answer.

If you want to know why there's a long history of economies and markets blowing past the boundaries of sanity, bouncing from boom to bust, bubble to crash, it's because so few people have Seinfeld's mentality. We insist on knowing where the top is, and the only way to find it is to keep pushing until we've gone too far, when we can look back and say, "Ah, I guess *that* was the top."

Are stocks overvalued? What is bitcoin worth? How high can Tesla go? You can't answer those questions with a formula. They're driven by whatever someone else is willing to pay for them in any given moment—how they feel, what they want to believe, and how persuasive the storytellers are. And the stories change all the time. They can't be predicted any more than you can predict what kind of mood you'll be in three years from now.

If an investment might have potential to go higher, somebody somewhere will test it to find out. People's desire to get rich far exceeds the number of easy and obvious opportunities. So if you put up a sign that says "There might be an opportunity in this box," somebody will always open the box. Which is to say: we have to identify where the top is.

That's why markets don't stay within the limits of sanity, and why they always overdose on pessimism and optimism.

They have to.

The only way to know we've exhausted all potential opportunity from markets—the only way to identify the top—is to push them not only past the point where the numbers stop making sense, but beyond the stories people believe about those numbers.

When a tire company develops a new tire and wants to know its limitations, the process is simple. They put it on a car and run it until it blows up. Markets, desperate to know the limits of what other investors can endure, do the same thing.

Always been the case, always will be.

There are two things you can do about it.

One is accepting that crazy doesn't mean broken. Crazy is normal; *beyond the point of crazy* is normal.

Every few years there seems to be a declaration that markets don't work anymore—that they're all speculation or detached from fundamentals. But it's always been that way. People haven't lost their minds; they're just searching for the boundaries of what other investors are willing to believe.

The second is realizing the power of enough. Being more like Seinfeld. Investor Chamath Palihapitiya was once asked about earning the highest returns, and remarked:

> I would really love to just compound at fifteen percent per year.
> Because if I can do that for fifty years that's just enormous.
> Just slow and steady against hard problems.

Maybe there's more potential out there, but it's fine to say, "You know what, I'm pretty happy with this level of risk and I'm fine just watching this game play out." Not everyone can do it—and markets on average can never do it—but more of us should try.

Next, let's talk about another wild problem: people's tendency to want to make good things bigger and faster.

Too Much,
Too Soon,
Too Fast

A good idea on steroids quickly
becomes a terrible idea.

W ARREN BUFFETT ONCE joked that you can't make a baby
in one month by getting nine women pregnant.

You'd be surprised, though, how common it is for people to
attempt to speed up a process beyond what it can handle.

Whenever people discover something valuable—particularly
a lucrative investment or a special skill—there is a tendency to
ask, "Great, but can I have it all faster?" Can we push it twice as
hard? Can we make it twice the size? Can we squeeze some more
juice out of it?

It's a natural question, and understandable.

But the history of taking something valuable and pushing it
too far, trying to make it go too fast, and asking too much, is long.

Most things have a natural size and speed and backfire quickly when you push them beyond that.

Let me tell you about Robert Wadlow. He was enormous, the largest human ever known.

A pituitary gland abnormality bombarded Wadlow's body with growth hormone, leading to staggering size. He was six feet tall at age seven, seven feet tall by age eleven, and when he died at twenty-two stood an inch shy of nine feet, weighed five hundred pounds, and wore size 37 shoes. His hand was a foot wide.

He was what fiction would portray as a superhuman athlete, capable of running faster, jumping higher, lifting more weight, and crushing more bad guys than any normal person. A real-life Paul Bunyan.

But that was not Wadlow's life at all.

He required steel leg braces to stand and a cane to walk. His walk wasn't much more than a limp, requiring tremendous effort. What few videos of Wadlow exist show a man whose movements are strained and awkward. He was rarely seen standing on his own, and usually leaned on a wall for support. So much pressure was put on his legs that near the end of his life he had little feeling below his knees. Had Wadlow lived longer and kept growing, casual walking would have caused his leg bones to break. What actually killed him was nearly as grim: Wadlow had high blood pressure in his legs due to his heart straining to pump blood around his enormous body, which caused an ulcer, which led to a deadly infection.

You can't triple the size of a human and expect triple the performance—the mechanics don't work like that. Huge animals tend to have short, squatty legs (rhinos), or extremely long legs relative to their torso (giraffes). Wadlow grew too large given the structure of the human body. There are limits to scaling.

Writing before Wadlow's time, biologist J. B. S. Haldane once showed how many things this scaling issue applies to.

A flea can jump two feet in the air, an athletic man about four. But if a flea were as large as a man, it would not be able to jump thousands of feet—it doesn't scale like that. Air resistance would be far greater for the giant flea, and the amount of energy needed to jump a given height is proportional to weight. If a flea were a thousand times its normal size, its hop might increase from two feet to perhaps six, Haldane assumed.

A human exiting a bathtub has perhaps a pound of water dripping off them—no big deal. A wet mouse, on the other hand, must lug around its body weight in excess water, and a wet fly is effectively pinned to the ground. The same action at different sizes produces massively different problems.

"For every type of animal there is a most convenient size, and a change in size inevitably carries with it a change of form," Haldane wrote.

A most convenient size.

A proper state where things work well but break when you try to scale them to a different size or speed.

It applies to so many things in life.

———————

A good summary of investing history is that stocks pay a fortune in the long run but seek punitive damages when you demand to be paid sooner.

Here's how often the U.S. stock market has generated a positive return based on how long you held stocks for.

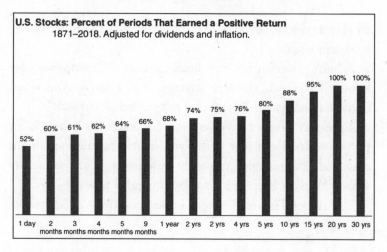

U.S. Stocks: Percent of Periods That Earned a Positive Return
1871–2018. Adjusted for dividends and inflation.

One way to think about this chart is that there's a "most convenient" investing time horizon—probably somewhere around ten years or more. That's the period in which markets nearly always reward your patience. The more your time horizon compresses, the more you rely on luck and tempt ruin.

Go down the list of historical investing blunders, and I'm telling you, no less than 90 percent of them are caused by investors trying to compress this natural, "most convenient" time horizon.

The same thing happens to companies.

Starbucks had 425 stores in 1994, its twenty-third year in existence. In 1999 it *opened* 625 new stores. By 2007 it was opening 2,500 stores per year—a new coffee shop every four hours.

One thing led to another. The need to hit growth targets eventually elbowed out rational analysis. Examples of Starbucks saturation became a joke. Same-store sales growth fell by half as the rest of the economy boomed.

Howard Schultz wrote to senior management in 2007: "In order to go from less than 1,000 stores to 13,000 stores we have had to make a series of decisions that, in retrospect, have led to the watering down of the Starbucks experience." Starbucks closed six hundred stores in 2008 and laid off twelve thousand employees. Its stock fell 73 percent, which was dreadful even by 2008 standards.

Schultz wrote in his 2011 book *Onward*: "Growth, we now know all too well, is not a strategy. It is a tactic. And when undisciplined growth became a strategy, we lost our way."

There was a most convenient size for Starbucks—there is for all businesses. Push past it and you realize that revenue might scale but disappointed customers scale faster, in the same way Robert Wadlow became a giant but struggled to walk.

Tire tycoon Harvey Firestone understood this well, and wrote in 1926:

> It does not pay to try to get the business all at once. In the first place, you can't get it, so a good deal of your money is thrown away. In the second place, if you did get it, the factory could not handle it. And in the third place, if you did get it, you could not hold it. A company that gets business too quickly acts just about as a boy does who gets money too quickly.

Corporate mergers often fall for the same trap. Growth by acquisition often occurs when management wants faster growth than customers think the business deserves. The customers' desire is likely closer to the "most convenient" size of a business, and force-feeding beyond that point leads to all kinds of disappointment.

Nassim Taleb says he's a libertarian at the federal level, a Republican at the state level, a Democrat at the local level, and a socialist at the family level. People handle risk and responsibility in totally different ways when a group scales from 4 people to 100 to 100,000 to 100 million.

Same for corporate culture. A management style that works brilliantly at a ten-person company can destroy a thousand-person company, which is a hard lesson to learn when some companies grow that fast in a few short years. Travis Kalanick, the former CEO of Uber, is a great example. No one but him was capable of growing the company early on, and anyone but him was needed as the company matured. I don't think that's a flaw, just a reflection that some things don't scale.

There are endless similar examples in nature, most highlighting that a good idea sped up too fast quickly becomes a terrible idea.

———————

Most young tree saplings spend their early decades under the shade of their mother's canopy. Limited sunlight means they grow slowly. Slow growth leads to dense, hard wood.

But something interesting happens if you plant a tree in an open field: free from the shade of bigger trees, the sapling gorges on sunlight and grows fast.

Fast growth leads to soft, airy wood that never had time to densify. And soft, airy wood is a breeding ground for fungus and disease. "A tree that grows quickly rots quickly and therefore never has a chance to grow old," forester Peter Wohlleben wrote. Haste makes waste.

Or consider animal growth.

Take two groups of identical baby fish. Put one in abnormally cold water, the other in abnormally warm water. There's a certain temperature on either end that does something interesting: Fish living in cold water will grow slower than normal, while those in warm water will grow faster than normal.

Put both groups back in regular-temperature water and they'll eventually converge to become normal, full-sized adults.

But then something astounding happens.

Fish with slowed-down growth in their early years go on to live 30 percent longer than average. Those with artificial, supercharged growth early on die 15 percent earlier than average.

That's what a team of biologists from Glasgow University once found.

The cause isn't complicated. Supercharged growth can lead to tissue damage and, as the biologists put it, "may only be achieved by diversion of resources away from maintenance and repair of damaged biomolecules." Slowed-down growth does the opposite, "allowing an increased allocation to maintenance and repair."

"You might well expect a machine built in haste to fail quicker than one put together carefully and methodically, and our study suggests that this may be true for bodies too," Neil Metcalfe, one of the researchers, said.

Growth is good, if only because runts eventually get eaten. But forced growth, accelerated growth, *artificial* growth—that tends to backfire.

Robert Greene writes: "The greatest impediment to creativity is your impatience, the almost inevitable desire to hurry up the process, express something, and make a splash."

An important thing about this topic is that most great things in life—from love to careers to investing—gain their value from two things: patience and scarcity. Patience to let something grow, and scarcity to admire what it grows into.

But what are two of the most common tactics when people pursue something great? Trying to make it faster and bigger.

It's always been a problem, and always will be.

Same as ever.

In the next chapter, let's look at another timeless topic: how, when, and why people find motivation.

When the Magic Happens

**Stress focuses your attention
in ways that good times can't.**

A CONSTANT TRUTH YOU see throughout history is that the biggest changes and the most important innovations don't happen when everyone is happy and things are going well. They tend to occur during, and after, a terrible event. When people are a little panicked, shocked, worried, and when the consequences of not acting quickly are too painful to bear.

The Triangle Shirtwaist Factory fire was one of the biggest tragedies in New York City's history.

On March 25, 1911, a fire broke out in a garment factory staffed with hundreds of mostly immigrant women—many of them young teenagers, few older than age twenty-two.

Within minutes, the factory was nearly engulfed.

Firefighters were at the scene soon after. But their ladders could only reach as high as the sixth floor—four stories below the helpless workers.

"Everybody was running, trying to get out," said Bessie Cohen, a survivor of the fire.

Panicked workers crowded in the building's windows, searching for the last gasps of oxygen.

Crowds began congregating on the streets below. What they saw next, no one would ever forget.

One passerby said something that looked like a burning bale of old clothes fell out of the building and hit the ground with a thud. Another commented that they must be throwing burning clothes out the window to try to stop the fire.

With more thuds, it became apparent that factory workers were jumping to their death.

First one, then a few more, then dozens.

"Thud-dead, thud-dead, thud-dead, thud-dead," is how one witness described it.

The doors and fire escapes of the factory had been locked shut to prevent workers from taking unscheduled breaks. When a freight elevator stopped working, jumping became the only way out of the inferno.

"There was this beautiful little girl, my friend, Dora," Cohen recalled. "I remember her face before she jumped."

The whole tragedy was over in less than thirty minutes. One hundred and forty-six workers died.

Later that evening, a woman named Frances Perkins, who witnessed the fire from the street below, described to a reporter what she saw.

"They came down in twos and threes, jumping together in a kind of desperate hope," Perkins said. "The life nets were broken. The firemen kept shouting for them not to jump. But they had no choice; the flames were right behind them."

Thirty years later, Perkins would be appointed by

President Franklin Roosevelt as secretary of labor—the first woman member of a presidential cabinet.

Appalled by what she witnessed at the Triangle fire, and how preventable the deaths could have been had the employees had better working conditions—as simple as fire escapes and unlocked doors—Perkins and countless others devoted much of the rest of their lives to fighting for workers' rights.

"We banded ourselves together," Perkins wrote, "moved by a sense of stricken guilt, to prevent this kind of disaster from ever happening again." She called it "a never-to-be-forgotten reminder of why I had to spend my life fighting conditions that could permit such a tragedy."

The Triangle fire tragedy was in many ways the beginning of a workers' rights movement that transformed the twentieth century.

Looking back almost half a century after the fire, Perkins said that the New Deal—the 1930s economic policies to remake the U.S. economy with an eye toward workers' rights—began in spirit on March 25, 1911, the day of the Triangle fire.

Stress, pain, discomfort, shock, and disgust—for all its tragic downsides, it's also when the magic happens.

Cars and airplanes are two of the biggest innovations of modern times.

But there's an interesting thing about their early years.

Few looked at early cars and said, "Oh, there's a thing I can commute to work in."

Few saw a plane and said, "Aha, I can use that to get to my next vacation."

It took decades for people to see that potential.

What they did say early on was, "Can we mount a machine gun on that? Can we drop bombs out of it?"

Adolphus Greely was one of the first people outside the car

industry to realize the "horseless carriage" could be useful. Greely, a brigadier general, purchased three cars in 1899—almost a decade before Ford's Model T—for the U.S. Army to experiment with.

In one of its first mentions of automobiles, the *Los Angeles Times* wrote about General Greely's purchase:

> It can be used for the transportation of light artillery such as machine guns. It can be utilized for the carrying of equipment, ammunition and supplies; for taking the wounded to the rear, and, in general, for most of the purposes to which the power of mules and horses is now applied.

Nine years later, the *Los Angeles Times* did an interview with young brothers Wilbur and Orville Wright, who talked about the prospects of their new flying machine:

> The utility of the airship, they think, will lie entirely in its advantage as a reconnoitering agent in time of war. They have no desire to sell their invention to a private company but desire to have the War Department at Washington take it up.

The Wrights had reason to believe this was true. Their only real customer in their early years—the only group to show interest in airplanes—was the U.S. Army, which purchased the first "flyer" in 1908.

The army's early interest in cars and planes wasn't a fluke of lucky foresight. Go down the list of big innovations, and militaries show up repeatedly.

Radar.

Atomic energy.

The internet.

Microprocessors.

Jets.

Rockets.

Antibiotics.

Interstate highways.

Helicopters.

GPS.

Digital photography.

Microwave ovens.

Synthetic rubber.

They all either came directly from, or were heavily influenced by, the military.

Why?

Are militaries home to the greatest technical visionaries? The most talented engineers?

Perhaps.

But more importantly, they're home to Really Big Problems That Need to Be Solved Right Now.

Innovation is driven by incentives, which come in many forms.

On one hand there's "If I don't figure this out I might get fired." That will get your brain in gear.

Then there's "If I figure this out I might help people and make a lot of money." That will produce creative sparks.

Then there's what militaries have dealt with: "If we don't figure this out right now we're all going to die and Adolf Hitler might take over the world." That will fuel the most incredible problem-solving and innovation in the shortest period of time that the world has ever seen.

Frederick Lewis Allen describes the burst of scientific progress that took place during World War II:

> What the government, through its Office of Scientific Research and Development and other agencies, was constantly saying during the war was, in effect: "Is this discovery or that one of any possible war value? If so, then develop it and put it to use, and damn the expense!"

Militaries are engines of innovation because they occasionally deal with problems so important—so urgent, so vital—that money and manpower are removed as obstacles, and those involved collaborate in ways that are hard to emulate during calm times.

You cannot compare the incentives of Silicon Valley coders trying to get you to click on ads to Manhattan Project physicists trying to end a war that threatened the country's existence. You can't even compare their capabilities.

The same people with the same intelligence have wildly different potential under different circumstances.

And the circumstances that tend to produce the biggest innovations are those that cause people to be worried, scared, and eager to move quickly because their future depends on it.

"Nothing can become truly resilient when everything goes right," Shopify founder Toby Lütke said.

"The excess energy released from overreaction to setbacks is what innovates!" wrote Nassim Taleb.

Stress focuses your attention in ways good times can't. It kills procrastination and indecision, taking what you need to get done and shoving it so close to your face that you have no choice but to pursue it, right now and to the best of your ability.

During World War II an unnamed U.S. soldier was interviewed by a newspaper. Asked what he was thinking during combat, the soldier replied: "I was hoping to remember to stay afraid because that is the best way to stay alive and not make careless mistakes."

It's good advice and a smart insight that applies to many things.

The 1930s were a disaster, one of the darkest periods in American history.

Almost a quarter of Americans were out of work in 1932. The stock market fell 89 percent.

Those two economic stories dominate the decade's attention, and they should.

But there's another story about the 1930s that rarely gets mentioned: it was, by far, the most productive and technologically progressive decade in U.S. history.

The number of problems people solved, and the ways they discovered how to build stuff more efficiently, is a forgotten story of the '30s that helps explain a lot of why the rest of the twentieth century was so prosperous.

Here are the numbers: total factor productivity—that's economic output relative to the number of hours people worked and the amount of money invested in the economy—hit levels not seen before or since.

Economist Alex Field wrote that by 1941 the U.S. economy was producing 40 percent more output than it had in 1929, with virtually no increase in the total number of hours worked. Everyone simply became staggeringly more productive.

A couple of things happened during this period that are worth paying attention to, because they explain why this happened when it did.

Take cars. The 1920s was the era of the automobile. The number of cars on the road in America jumped from one million in 1912 to twenty-nine million by 1929.

But roads were a different story. Cars were sold in the 1920s faster than roads were built.

That changed in the 1930s when road construction, driven by the New Deal's Public Works Administration, took off.

Spending on road construction went from 2 percent of GDP in 1920 to over 6 percent in 1933 (versus less than 1 percent today). The Department of Highway Transportation tells a story of how quickly projects began:

> Construction began on August 5, 1933, in Utah on the first highway project under the act. By August 1934, 16,330 miles of new roadway projects were completed.

What this did to productivity is hard to overstate. The Pennsylvania Turnpike, as one example, cut travel times between Pittsburgh and Harrisburg by 70 percent. The Golden Gate Bridge, built in 1933, opened up Marin County, which had previously been accessible from San Francisco only by ferryboat.

Multiply those kinds of leaps across the nation and the 1930s was the decade that transportation blossomed in the United States. It was the last link that made the century-old railroad network truly efficient, creating last-mile service that connected the world.

Electrification also surged in the 1930s, particularly to rural Americans left out of the urban electrification of the 1920s.

The New Deal's Rural Electrification Administration (REA) brought power to farms in what may have been the decade's only positive development in regions that were economically devastated. The number of rural American homes with electricity rose from less than 10 percent in 1935 to nearly 50 percent by 1945.

It is hard to fathom, but it was not long ago—during some of our lifetimes and most of our grandparents'—that a substantial portion of America was literally dark. Franklin Roosevelt said in a speech on the REA:

Electricity is no longer a luxury. It is a definite necessity. . . . In our homes it serves not only for light, but it can become the willing servant of the family in countless ways. It can relieve the drudgery of the housewife and lift the great burden off the shoulders of the hardworking farmer.

Electricity becoming a "willing servant"—introducing washing machines, vacuum cleaners, and refrigerators—freed up hours of household labor in a way that let female workforce participation rise. It's a trend that lasted more than half a century and is a key driver of both twentieth-century growth and gender equality.

Another productivity surge of the 1930s came from everyday people forced by necessity to find more bang for their buck.

The first supermarket opened in 1930. The traditional way of purchasing food was to walk from your butcher, who served you from behind a counter, to the bakery, who served you from behind a counter, to a produce stand, who took your order. Combining everything under one roof and making customers pick it from the shelves themselves was a way to make the economics of selling food work during a time when a quarter of the nation was unemployed.

Laundromats were also invented in the 1930s after sales of individual washing machines fell; they marketed themselves as washing machine rentals.

Factories of all kinds looked at bludgeoned sales and said, "What must we do to survive?" The answer often was to build the kind of assembly line Henry Ford introduced to the world in the previous decade.

Output per hour in factories had grown 21 percent during the 1920s. "During the Depression decade of 1930–1940—when many plants were shut down or working part time," Frederick Lewis Allen wrote, "there was intense pressure for efficiency and economy—it had increased by an amazing 41 percent."

"The trauma of the Great Depression did not slow down the American invention machine," economist Robert Gordon wrote. "If anything, the pace of innovation picked up."

Driving knowledge work in the '30s was the fact that more young people stayed in school because they had nothing else to do. High school graduation surged during the Depression to levels not seen again until the 1960s.

All of this—the better factories, the new ideas, the educated workers—became vital in 1941 when America entered the war and became the Allied manufacturing engine.

The big question is whether the technical leap of the 1930s could have happened without the devastation of the Depression.

And I think the answer is no—at least not to the extent that it occurred.

You could never push through something like the New Deal without an economy so wrecked that people were desperate to try anything to fix it.

It's doubtful that business owners and entrepreneurs would so urgently have found new efficiencies without the record threat of business failure.

Managers looking at their employees and saying, "Go try something new. Blow up the playbook, I don't care," is not something that gets said when the economy is booming and the outlook is bright.

Big, fast changes happen only when they're forced by necessity.

World War II began on horseback in 1939 and ended with nuclear fission in 1945. NASA was created in 1958, two weeks after the Soviets launched Sputnik, and landed on the moon just eleven years later. Stuff like that rarely happens that fast without fear as a motivator.

Same with commercial airplanes. Flying is as safe as it is because after every accident comes an intense learn-and-fix process that reduces the odds of similar future accidents.

The same thing occurred in the 2000s, when an oil shock in 2008 that made prices surge incentivized oil companies to innovate on drilling techniques, which brought American oil production to record highs. Would the innovation boom have occurred without the previous crisis? Almost certainly not.

Same during COVID-19, when a generational risk and panic set off an astounding development and production of new vaccines.

Vannevar Bush, who ran the U.S. Office of Scientific Research and Development during World War II, controversially suggested the medical advances that came about from the war—most notably the production and use of antibiotics—may have saved more lives than were lost during the war.

It's so difficult to imagine these upsides as a crisis is happening. But time and again throughout history, the upsides indeed occur.

———

There's an obvious limit to stress-induced innovation.

There's a delicate balance between helpful stress and crippling disaster. The latter prevents innovation as resources are sapped and people turn their attention from getting out of a crisis to merely surviving it.

And perhaps just as important is what happens when we have the opposite. When everything is great—when wealth is flush, when the outlook is bright, when responsibility is low, and threats appear gone—you get some of the worst, dumbest, least-productive human behavior.

President Richard Nixon once observed:

> The unhappiest people of the world are those in the international watering places like the South Coast of France, and Newport, and Palm Springs, and Palm Beach. Going to parties every night. Playing golf every afternoon. Drinking too much. Talking too much. Thinking too little. Retired. No purpose.

So while there are those that would totally disagree with this and say "Gee, if I could just be a millionaire! That would be the most wonderful thing." If I could just not have to work every day, if I could just be out fishing or hunting or playing golf or traveling, that would be the most wonderful life in the world—they don't know life. Because what makes life mean something is purpose. A goal. The battle, the struggle—even if you don't win it.

Entrepreneur Andrew Wilkinson echoed the same when he said, "Most successful people are just a walking anxiety disorder harnessed for productivity."

Investor Patrick O'Shaughnessy writes: "In my experience many of the most talented people I've met couldn't be described as happy. In fact there are probably more that could be described as 'tortured.'"

The fear, the pain, the struggle are motivators that positive feelings can never match.

That's a big takeaway from history, and it leads to a realization that will always be true: **Be careful what you wish for.**

A carefree and stress-free life sounds wonderful only until you recognize the motivation and progress it prevents. No one cheers for hardship—nor should they—but we should recognize that it's the most potent fuel of problem-solving, serving as both the root of what we enjoy today and the seed of opportunity for what we'll enjoy tomorrow.

Next, a story of Dwight Eisenhower's worst day, and the timeless topic of miracles and disasters.

Overnight Tragedies and Long-Term Miracles

Good news comes from compounding, which
always takes time, but bad news comes
from a loss in confidence or a catastrophic
error that can occur in a blink of an eye.

A N IMPORTANT FACT that explains a lot of things is that good news takes time but bad news tends to occur instantly.

Warren Buffett says it takes twenty years to build a reputation and five minutes to destroy one.

A lot of things work just like that.

It's a natural part of how the world works, driven by the fact that good news comes from compounding, which always takes time, but bad news comes from a loss in confidence or a catastrophic error that can occur in the blink of an eye.

Dwight Eisenhower ate a hamburger for lunch on September 23, 1955. Later that evening he complained of chest pain and told his wife the onions gave him heartburn. Then he began to panic. The president was having a massive heart attack. It could easily have killed him. If it had, Eisenhower would have joined more than seven hundred thousand Americans who died of heart disease that year.

What's happened since has been extraordinary. But few have paid attention.

The age-adjusted death rate per capita from heart disease has declined more than 70 percent since the 1950s, according to the National Institutes of Health.

So many Americans die of heart disease that cutting the fatality rate by 70 percent leads to a number of lives saved that is hard to comprehend.

Had the rate not declined—if we hadn't become better at treating heart disease and the mortality rate hadn't plateaued since the 1950s—twenty-five million more Americans would have died from heart disease over the last sixty-five years than actually did.

Twenty-five million!

Even in a single year the improvement is incredible: more than half a million fewer Americans now die of heart disease each year than if we hadn't made any improvements since the 1950s. That's a full football stadium saved every month.

How is this not a bigger story?

Why are we not shouting in the streets about how incredible this is and building statues for cardiologists?

I'll tell you why: because the improvement happened too slowly for anyone to notice.

The average annual decline in heart disease mortality between 1950 and 2014 was 1.5 percent per year.

How would you react if you saw a news headline that read,

"Heart Disease Deaths Decline 1.5% Last Year." You'd yawn and move on.

So that's what we've done.

We do it all the time. The most important things come from compounding. But compounding takes awhile, so it's easy to ignore.

New technologies take years or decades for people to even notice, then years or decades more for people to accept and put to use. Show me a new technology that was immediately recognized for its full potential and instantly adopted by the masses. It doesn't exist. A lot of pessimism is fueled by the fact that it often looks like we haven't innovated in years—but that's usually because it takes years to notice a new innovation. This is true even in hard sciences: Historian David Wooton says it took two hundred years from discovering germs to the medical acceptance that germs cause disease, another thirty years to discover antisepsis, and another sixty years before penicillin was in use.

Same for economic growth.

Real GDP per capita increased eightfold in the last hundred years. America of the 1920s had the same real per-capita GDP as Turkmenistan does today. Our growth over the last century has been unbelievable. But GDP growth averages about 3 percent per year, which is easy to ignore in any given year, decade, or lifetime. Americans over age fifty have seen real GDP per person at least double since they were born. But people don't remember the world when they were born. They remember the last few months, when progress is always invisible.

Same for careers, social progress, brands, companies, and relationships. Progress always takes time, often too much time to even notice it's happened.

But bad news?

It's not shy or subtle. It comes instantly, so fast that it overwhelms your attention and you can't look away.

Pearl Harbor and September 11 are probably the two biggest news events of the last hundred years. Both took about an hour to play out, start to finish.

It took less than thirty days for most people to go from never having heard of COVID-19 to it upending their life.

It took less than fifteen months for Lehman Brothers—a 158-year-old company—to go from an all-time high to bankrupt. Same with Enron, Fannie Mae and Freddie Mac, Nokia, Bernie Madoff, Muammar Gaddafi, Notre-Dame Cathedral, and the Soviet Union. Things that thrived for decades can be ruined in minutes. There is no equivalent in the other direction.

There's a good reason why.

Growth always fights against competition that slows its rise. New ideas fight for attention, business models fight incumbents, skyscrapers fight gravity. There's always a headwind. But everyone gets out of the way of decline. Some might try to step in and slow the fall, but it doesn't attract masses of outsiders who rush in to push back in the other direction the way progress does.

———

Tens of billions of individual steps have to go right in the correct order to create a human. But only one thing has to happen to cause its demise.

After just five weeks a human embryo has a brain, a beating heart, a pancreas, a liver, and a gallbladder. By birth, a baby has 100 billion neurons, 250 trillion synapses, 11 cooperating organ systems, and a personality. It's staggeringly complex.

Death, on the other hand, is simple. Most deaths—trauma, heart disease, stroke, some cancers, infections, drug overdoses— are caused by blood and oxygen deficiencies. That's it. A disease itself might be complex, but the fatal strike is not enough blood and oxygen getting to where it's needed.

Making a human: incomprehensibly complex.

The death of a human: really simple.

On a similar note, author Yuval Noah Harari writes: "To enjoy peace, we need almost everyone to make good choices. By contrast, a poor choice by just one side can lead to war."

The idea of "complex to make, simple to break" is everywhere. Construction requires skilled engineers; demolition requires only a sledgehammer. Even when something doesn't break easily, the thing that could break it is usually simpler than whatever made it.

The irony is that growth and progress are way more powerful than setbacks. But setbacks will always get more attention because of how fast they occur. So slow progress amid a drumbeat of bad news is the normal state of affairs. It's not an easy thing to get used to, but it'll always be with us.

A couple things stick out here.

A lot of progress and good news concerns things that didn't happen, whereas virtually all bad news is about what did occur.

Good news is the deaths that didn't take place, the diseases you didn't get, the wars that never happened, the tragedies avoided, and the injustices prevented. That's hard for people to contextualize or even imagine, let alone measure.

But bad news is visible. More than visible, it's in your face. It's the terrorist attack, the war, the car accident, the pandemic, the stock market crash, and the political battle you can't look away from.

It is so easy to discount how much progress is achievable.

If I were to say, "What are the odds the average American will be twice as rich fifty years from now?" it sounds preposterous. The odds seem very low. *Twice* as rich as they are today? *Doubling* what we already have? It seems too ambitious.

But then if I said, "What are the odds we can achieve 1.4 percent average annual growth for the next fifty years?" I almost sound like a pessimist. *One percent? That's it?*

But those numbers, of course, are the same.

It's always been like that, and always will be.

On a related topic: Let me share a story about nuclear bombs to show how easy it is to discount risks.

Tiny and Magnificent

When little things compound into extraordinary things.

A COMMON THEME IN history is that people assume the biggest companies, nations, and innovations pose the biggest threats and create the biggest opportunities.

But that's usually not how it works.

A 2010 Yale study showed that one of the leading causes of the increase in obesity is not necessarily people eating larger meals; it's eating more small snacks throughout the day.

It's a good example of how lots of things work.

Most catastrophes come from a series of tiny risks—each of which is easy to ignore—that multiply and compound into something huge. The opposite is true: Most amazing things happen when something tiny and insignificant compounds into something extraordinary.

The Soviets once built a nuclear bomb fifteen hundred times stronger than the one dropped on Hiroshima.

Called Tsar Bomba (king of bombs), it was ten times more powerful than every conventional bomb dropped during World War II combined. When tested in Russia, its fireball was seen six hundred miles away. Its mushroom cloud went forty-two miles into the sky.

Historian John Lewis Gaddis wrote:

> The island over which the explosion took place was literally leveled, not only of snow but also of rocks, so that it looked like an immense skating rink. One estimate calculated . . . the resulting firestorm would have engulfed an area the size of the state of Maryland.

The first nuclear bomb was developed to end World War II. Within a decade we had enough bombs to end the world—all of it.

But there was a weird silver lining to how deadly these bombs were: countries were unlikely to use them in battle because they raised the stakes so high. Wipe out an enemy's capital city and they'll do the same to you sixty seconds later—so why bother? John F. Kennedy said neither country wanted "a war that would leave not one Rome intact but two Carthages destroyed."

By 1960 we got around this predicament by going the other way. We built smaller, less deadly nuclear bombs.

One, called Davy Crockett, was 650 times less powerful than the bomb dropped on Hiroshima and could be fired from the back of a Jeep. We built nuclear landmines that could fit in a backpack, with a warhead the size of a shoebox.

These tiny nukes felt more responsible, less risky. We could use them without ending the world.

But they backfired.

Small nuclear bombs were more likely to actually be used in

combat. That was their whole purpose. They lowered the bar of justified use.

It changed the game, all for the worse.

The risk was that a country would "responsibly" use a tiny nuclear weapon in battle, starting a retaliatory escalation that opened the door to launching one of the big bombs.

Neither country would start a war with a big bomb. But would they launch a small one? Probably. And would a small bomb justify retaliating with a big one? Yes.

So the small bombs increased the odds of the big bombs being used.

Small risks weren't the alternative to big risks; they were the trigger.

Soviet missiles in Cuba during the Cuban Missile Crisis were four thousand times less powerful than *Tsar Bomba*. But if the Soviets had launched even one of them, according to Secretary of Defense Robert McNamara, there would have been a "99 percent probability" that America would have retaliated with its full nuclear force.

Robert Oppenheimer, the physicist who helped create the atomic bomb, was guilt-stricken about its destructiveness and pushed for smaller nukes to reduce the risk. He later admitted that was a mistake, because it increased the odds of a large nuclear attack.

Big risks are easy to overlook because they're just a chain reaction of small events, each of which is easy to shrug off. So people always underestimate the odds of big risks.

We've seen it happen time after time.

No one in 1929 thought there would be a Great Depression. You'd be laughed away if you warned in 1929 that the stock market was about to fall nearly 90 percent and unemployment rise to 25 percent.

People weren't complacent. The late 1920s saw an overvalued

stock market, real estate speculation, and poor farm maintenance. That was obvious. It was well-documented. It was discussed. But so what? None of those things are a big deal in isolation.

It wasn't until they happened at the same time, and fed off one another, that they turned into the Great Depression.

The stock market falls, the boss loses his savings, he lays people off, those people default on their mortgage, and the bank goes under. When banks fail, people lose their savings. When they lose their savings, they stop spending. When they stop spending, businesses fail. When businesses fail, banks fail. When banks fail, people lose their savings—and so on endlessly.

Same thing with COVID-19.

Its initial impact was catastrophic, seemingly out of the blue.

But we didn't get hit with a single, one-in-billions risk. What happened—and I can say this only with hindsight—was a bunch of small risks colliding and multiplying at once.

A new virus transferred to humans (something that has happened forever), and those humans interacted with other people (of course). It was a mystery for a while (understandable), and then bad news was likely suppressed (bad, but common). Other countries thought it would be contained (standard denial), and didn't act fast enough (bureaucracy). We weren't prepared (overoptimism), and could respond only with blunt-force lockdowns (panic, do what you gotta do).

None of those on their own are surprising. But combined they turned into a disaster.

The Tenerife airport disaster in 1977 is the deadliest aircraft accident in history. The error was stunning. One plane took off while another was still on the runway, and the two Boeing 747s collided, killing 583 people on a runway on the Spanish island.

In the aftermath authorities wondered how such an egregious catastrophe could occur. One postmortem study explained exactly how: "Eleven separate coincidences and mistakes, most of them minor . . . had to fall precisely into place" for the crash to occur. Lots of tiny mistakes added up to a huge one.

It's good to always assume the world will break about once per decade, because historically it has. The breakages feel like low-probability events, so it's common to think they won't keep happening. But they do, again and again, because they're actually just smaller high-probability events compounding off one another.

That isn't intuitive, so we'll discount big risks like we always have.

And of course, the same thing happens in the other direction.

—————

The most astounding force in the universe is obvious. It's evolution. The thing that developed single-cell organisms into humans who can read this book on an iPad with a terabyte of storage. The thing that's responsible for 20/20 vision and flying birds and immune systems.

Nothing else in science can blow your mind more than what evolution has accomplished.

Biologist Leslie Orgel used to say, "Evolution is cleverer than you are," because whenever a critic says, "Evolution could never do that," they usually just lacked imagination.

It's also easy to underestimate because of basic math.

Evolution's superpower is not just selecting favorable traits. That part is so tedious, and if it's all you focus on you'll be skeptical and confused. Most species' change in any millennia is so trivial it's unnoticeable.

The real magic of evolution is that it's been selecting traits for 3.8 billion years.

The time, not the little changes, is what moves the needle. Take minuscule changes and compound them by 3.8 billion years and you get results that are indistinguishable from magic.

That's the real lesson from evolution: If you have a big number in the exponent slot, you do not need extraordinary change to deliver extraordinary results. It's not intuitive, but it's so powerful.

"The greatest shortcoming of the human race is our inability to understand the exponential function," physicist Albert Bartlett used to say.

A lot of things work like that.

An area where we commonly see this shortcoming in action is investing.

Investor Howard Marks once talked about an investor whose annual results were never ranked in the top quartile, but over a fourteen-year period he was in the top 4 percent of all investors. If he keeps those mediocre returns up for another ten years he may be in the top 1 percent of his peers—one of the greatest of his generation despite being unremarkable in any given year.

So much focus in investing is on what people can do right now, this year, maybe next year. "What are the best returns I can earn?" seems like such an intuitive question to ask.

But like evolution, that's not where the magic happens.

If you understand the math behind compounding you realize the most important question is not "How can I earn the highest returns?" It's "What are the best returns I can sustain for the longest period of time?"

Little changes compounded for a long time create extraordinary changes.

Same as ever.

Next, we'll look at the dangers of overconfidence.

Elation
and Despair

**Progress requires optimism and
pessimism to coexist.**

OPTIMISM AND PESSIMISM are so hard to deal with.
Pessimism is more intellectually seductive than optimism
and captures more of our attention. It's vital for survival, helping
us prepare for risks before they arrive.

But optimism is equally essential. The belief that things can
be, and will be, better even when the evidence is murky is one of
the most essential parts of everything from maintaining a sound
relationship to making a long-term investment.

A big thing to know about how people think is that progress
requires optimism and pessimism to coexist.

They seem like conflicting mindsets, so it's more common for
people to prefer one or the other. But knowing how to balance
the two has always been, and always will be, one of life's most
important skills.

The best financial plan is to save like a pessimist and invest like an optimist. That idea—the belief that things will get better mixed with the reality that the path between now and then will be a continuous chain of setback, disappointment, surprise, and shock—shows up all over history, in all areas of life.

John McCain became the most famous Vietnam prisoner of war. But at the time, Admiral Jim Stockdale was the highest-ranking POW.

Stockdale was tortured routinely, and at one point attempted suicide out of fear he might break and give up sensitive military information.

Decades after he was released, Stockdale was asked in an interview about how depressing life in prison must have been. He pushed back and said, actually, it was never depressing at all. He never lost faith that he would prevail—that he'd be released and reunited with his family.

Pure optimism, it seems. Right?

Not really.

Stockdale was then asked who had the hardest time in prison. He said that was easy: "It was the optimists."

The prisoners who constantly said, "We're going to be home by Christmas" were the ones whose spirits were shattered when another Christmas came and went. "They died of a broken heart," Stockdale said.

There is a balance, he said, between needing unwavering faith that things will get better while accepting the reality of brutal facts, whatever they may be. Things will eventually get better. But we're not going home by Christmas.

That's the balance—planning like a pessimist and dreaming like an optimist.

That mix is counterintuitive, but it's so powerful when done right.

Remaining optimistic while accepting the reality of despair is fascinating to witness.

"The American dream" was a phrase first used by author James Truslow Adams in his 1931 book *The Epic of America*.

The timing is interesting, isn't it? It's hard to think of a year when the dream looked more broken than in 1931.

When Adams wrote that "a man by applying himself, by using the talents he has, by acquiring the necessary skills, can rise from lower to higher status, and that his family can rise with him," the unemployment rate was nearly 25 percent and wealth inequality was near the highest it had been in American history.

When he wrote of "that American dream of a better, richer, and happier life for all our citizens of every rank," food riots were breaking out across the country as the Great Depression ripped the economy to shreds.

When he wrote of "being able to grow to fullest development as men and women, unhampered by the barriers which had slowly been erected in older civilizations," schools were segregated and some states required literacy tests to vote.

At few points in American history had the idea of the American dream looked so false, so out of touch with the reality everyone faced.

Yet Adams's book surged in popularity. An optimistic phrase born during a dark period in American history became an overnight household motto.

One quarter of Americans being out of work in 1931 didn't ruin the idea of the American Dream. The stock market falling 89 percent—and bread lines across the country—didn't, either.

The American Dream actually may have gained popularity because things were so dire. You didn't have to see the American Dream to believe in it—and thank goodness, because in 1931 there was nothing to see. You just had to believe it was possible and then, boom, you felt a little better.

Psychologists Lauren Alloy and Lyn Yvonne Abramson have a theory I love called depressive realism. It's the idea that depressed people have a more accurate view of the world because they're more realistic about how risky and fragile life is.

The opposite of depressive realism is "blissfully unaware." It's what many of us suffer from. But we don't actually suffer from it, because it feels great. And the fact that it feels good is the fuel we need to wake up and keep working even when the world around us can be objectively awful, and pessimism abounds.

In 1984 Jane Pauley interviewed twenty-eight-year-old Bill Gates. "Some people call you a genius," Pauley said. "I know that might embarrass you but . . ."

Gates deadpans. No emotion. No response.

"OK, I guess that doesn't embarrass you," Pauley says with an awkward laugh.

Again, zero reaction from Gates.

Of course he was a genius. And he knew it.

Gates dropped out of college at nineteen because he thought a computer should be on every desk in every home. You only do that when you have relentless confidence in your abilities. Paul Allen once wrote about the first time he met Bill:

> You could tell three things about Bill Gates pretty quickly. He was really smart. He was really competitive; he wanted to show you how smart he was. And he was really, really persistent.

But there was another side to Bill Gates. It was almost paranoia, virtually the opposite of his unshakable confidence.

From the day he started Microsoft, he insisted on always

having enough cash in the bank to keep the company alive for twelve months with no revenue coming in.

In 1995 he was asked by Charlie Rose why he kept so much cash on hand. Things change so fast in technology that next year's business wasn't guaranteed, he said. "Including Microsoft's."

In 2007 he reflected:

> I was always worried because people who worked for me were older than me and had kids, and I always thought, "What if we don't get paid, will I be able to meet the payroll?"

Here again, optimism and confidence mixed with heavy pessimism. What Gates seems to get is that you can only be an optimist in the long run if you're pessimistic enough to survive the short run.

An important thing to recognize here is that optimism and pessimism exist on a spectrum.

At one end you have the pure optimist. They think everything is great, will always be great, and see all negativity as a character flaw. Part is rooted in ego: they're so confident in themselves they can't fathom anything going wrong.

At the other end you have the pure pessimists. They think everything is terrible, will always be terrible, and see all positivity as a character flaw. Part is rooted in ego: they have so little confidence in themselves they can't fathom anything going right. They're the polar opposite of the pure optimist, and just as detached from reality.

Both are equally dangerous, but either can seem the most logical if you view optimism and pessimism as black-and-white, like you need to be one or the other.

In the middle is the sweet spot, what I call the rational optimists: those who acknowledge that history is a constant chain of problems and disappointments and setbacks, but who remain optimistic because they know setbacks don't prevent eventual progress. They sound like hypocrites and flip-floppers, but often they're just looking further ahead than other people.

———————

The trick in any field—from finance to careers to relationships—is being able to survive the short-run problems so you can stick around long enough to enjoy the long-term growth.

Save like a pessimist and invest like an optimist.

Plan like a pessimist and dream like an optimist.

Those can seem like conflicting skills. And they are. It's intuitive to think you should either be an optimist or a pessimist. It's hard to realize there's a time and a place for both, and that the two can—and should—coexist. But it's what you see in almost every successful long-term endeavor.

The business that takes huge risks with new products, like an optimist, but is terrified of short-term debt and always wants a big chunk of safety-net cash, like a pessimist.

The worker who turns down a lucrative opportunity because it might come at the expense of their reputation, which over the long run is far more valuable.

Same in investing. I wrote in my book *The Psychology of Money*: "More than I want big returns, I want to be financially unbreakable. And if I'm unbreakable I actually think I'll get the biggest returns, because I'll be able to stick around long enough for compounding to work wonders."

An important lesson from history is that the long run is usually pretty good and the short run is usually pretty bad. It takes effort to reconcile those two and learn how to manage them with what seem like conflicting skills. Those who can't usually end up either bitter pessimists or bankrupt optimists.

Moving right along. Now let's discuss another topic that's not intuitive: The more perfect you try to be, the worse you'll end up doing.

Casualties of
Perfection

There is a huge advantage to
being a little imperfect.

PEOPLE DON'T LIKE to leave opportunities on the table.
A common urge is to squeeze out as much efficiency and perfection as you can from whatever you're pursuing. It feels like the right thing to do, like you're maximizing your chances of success.

But there's a common downside to perfection that's so easy to overlook.

The key thing about evolution is that everything dies. Ninety-nine percent of species are already extinct; the rest will be eventually.

There is no perfect species, one adapted to everything at all times. The best any species can do is to be good at some things until the things it's not good at suddenly matter more. And then it dies.

A century ago a Russian biologist named Ivan Schmalhausen described how this works. A species that evolves to become very good at one thing tends to become vulnerable at another. A bigger lion can kill more prey, but it's also a larger target for hunters to shoot at. A taller tree captures more sunlight, but becomes vulnerable to wind damage. There is always some inefficiency.

So species rarely evolve to become perfect at *anything*, because perfecting one skill comes at the expense of another skill that will eventually be critical to survival. The lion could be bigger and catch more prey; the tree could be taller and get more sun. But they're not, because it would backfire.

So they're all a little imperfect.

Nature's answer is a lot of good enough, below-potential traits across all species. Biologist Anthony Bradshaw says that evolution's successes get all the attention, but its failures are equally important. And that's how it should be: Not maximizing your potential is actually the sweet spot in a world where perfecting one skill compromises another.

Evolution has spent 3.8 billion years testing and proving the idea that some inefficiency is good.

We know it's right.

So maybe we should pay more attention to it.

Many people strive for efficient lives, where no hour is wasted. But an overlooked skill that doesn't get enough attention is the idea that wasting time can be a great thing.

Psychologist Amos Tversky once said that "the secret to doing good research is always to be a little underemployed. You waste years by not being able to waste hours."

A successful person purposely leaving gaps of free time on their schedule to do nothing in particular can feel inefficient. And it is, so not many people do it.

But Tversky's point is that if your job is to be creative and think through tough problems, then time spent wandering around a park or aimlessly lounging on a couch might be your most valuable hours. A little inefficiency is wonderful.

Every person I've worked with comes back from vacation saying some variation of the same thing:

"Now that I had some time to think, I've realized . . ."

"With a few days to clear my mind, I figured out . . ."

"While I was away I got this great idea . . ."

The irony is that people can get some of their most important work done outside of work, when they're free to think and ponder. The struggle is that we take time off maybe once a year, without realizing that time to think is a key element of many jobs, and one that a traditional work schedule doesn't accommodate very well.

Not all jobs require creativity or critical thinking. But those that do function better with time devoted to wandering and being curious, in ways that are removed from scheduled work but actually help tackle your biggest work problems.

It's just hard to do that because we're set on the idea that a typical work day should be eight uninterrupted hours seated at your desk.

Tell your boss you found a trick that will make you more creative and productive, and she'll ask what you're waiting for. Tell her that your trick is taking a ninety-minute walk in the middle of the day, and she might say no, you need to work. Another way to put this is that a lot of workers have "thought jobs" without much time to think.

The New York Times once wrote of former Secretary of State George Shultz:

His hour of solitude was the only way he could find time to think about the strategic aspects of his job. Otherwise, he would be constantly pulled into moment-to-moment tactical issues, never able to focus on larger questions of the national interest.

Albert Einstein put it this way:

I take time to go for long walks on the beach so that I can listen to what is going on inside my head. If my work isn't going well, I lie down in the middle of a workday and gaze at the ceiling while I listen and visualize what goes on in my imagination.

Mozart felt the same way:

When I am traveling in a carriage or walking after a good meal or during the night when I cannot sleep—it is on such occasions that my ideas flow best and most abundantly.

This meshes with a Stanford study that showed walking increases creativity by 60 percent.

Someone once asked Charlie Munger what Warren Buffett's secret was. "I would say half of all the time he spends is sitting on his ass and reading." He has a lot of time to think.

The traditional eight-hour work schedule is great if your job is repetitive or physically constraining. But for the large and growing number of "thought jobs," it might not be.

You might be better off taking two hours in the morning to stay at home thinking about some big problem.

Or go for a long midday walk to ponder why something isn't working.

Or leave at 3:00 p.m. and spend the rest of the day envisioning a new strategy.

It's not about working less. It's the opposite: A lot of thought jobs basically never stop, and without structuring time to think and be curious, you wind up less efficient during the hours that are devoted to sitting at your desk cranking out work. This is the opposite of the concept of "hustle porn," where people want to look busy at all times because they think it's noble.

Nassim Taleb says, "My only measure of success is how much time you have to kill." More than a measure of success, I think it's a key ingredient. The most efficient calendar in the world—one where every minute is packed with productivity—comes at the expense of curious wandering and uninterrupted thinking, which eventually become the biggest contributors to success.

Another form of helpful inefficiency is a business whose operations have some slack built in.

Just-in-time manufacturing—where companies don't stock the parts they need to build products, relying instead on last-minute shipments of components—was the epitome of efficient operations over the last twenty years. Then COVID-19 hit, supply chains broke, and virtually every manufacturer found itself dreadfully short of what it needed.

The irony is deep: In 2022, during one of the biggest consumer spending booms in history, car companies had to shut down factories because they were short on chips, brakes, and paint. They had no room for error. Business's *goal* was no room for error—and it completely backfired. A little inefficiency across the whole supply chain would have been the sweet spot. Room for error is often viewed as a cost, an anchor, an inefficiency. But in the long run it can have some of the highest payoffs imaginable.

Same in investing. Cash is an inefficient drag during bull markets and as valuable as oxygen during bear markets. Leverage is the most efficient way to maximize your balance sheet and the easiest way to lose everything. Concentration is the best way to maximize returns, but diversification is the best way to increase the odds of owning a company capable of delivering returns. On and on.

If you're honest with yourself, you'll see that a little inefficiency is the ideal spot to be in.

Same with analysis. There's an investing quip that it's better to be approximately right than precisely wrong. But where does the intellectual effort go in the investment industry? Toward the pursuit of precisions—decimal-point exactness that deludes people into thinking they're not leaving opportunity on the table, when more often they are leaving no room for error for their analysis to be wrong.

Investing in your long-term future is of course great, because the odds that the economy will become more productive and more valuable are pretty good. But trying to predict the exact path we'll take to get there can be such a waste of resources.

I describe my forecasting model as "good enough."

I'm confident people will solve problems and become more productive over time.

I'm confident markets will allocate the rewards of that productivity to investors over time.

I'm confident in other people's overconfidence, so I know there will be mistakes and accidents and booms and busts along the way.

It's not detailed, but it's good enough.

When you keep forecasting that simple, you free up time and bandwidth for other activities. I like studying the investing behaviors that never change, and I'd never have the time to do that if I spent my day predicting what the economy will do next quarter. The same is true in virtually every field. The more precise you try to be, the less time you have to focus on big-picture rules that are probably more important. It's less about admitting that we can't forecast, and more about acknowledging that if your forecast is merely good enough, you can invest your time and resources more efficiently elsewhere.

Just like evolution, the key is realizing that the more perfect you try to become, the more vulnerable you generally are.

Next, one of the wildest stories I know. It's about another risk that's easy to ignore: the downside of shortcuts.

It's Supposed to Be Hard

Everything worth pursuing comes
with a little pain. The trick is
not minding that it hurts.

L ET ME SHARE a few ideas about the allure, and danger, of shortcuts.

Few stories make you wince as much as that of the Donner Party.

Eighty-seven people led by the Donner family left Springfield, Illinois, in 1846 for California, which was then seemingly a world away but held the promise of riches and a new beginning.

The journey was grueling and risky in the best of times, taking several months and under constant threat of attack from Native Americans, disease, and nasty weather.

Halfway through the trip the Donners, exhausted from months on the trail, took the advice of an Ohio explorer named Lansford Hastings, who convinced them they could shave perhaps three or four days off their trip by cutting through what is now Utah, bypassing the traditional and well-known trail through what is now southern Idaho.

Hastings was wrong in nearly every regard. The "shortcut" was far longer and more arduous than the traditional route, taking them through the scorching heat of the Great Salt Lake Desert in the middle of summer. The party nearly ran out of water, lost the majority of their oxen, and—most critically—added a month to their journey.

That delay could not have been more catastrophic.

The Donner Party would now cross the Sierra Nevada mountains near Lake Tahoe in the middle of winter, instead of the late fall as first planned. The winter of 1847 turned out to be one of the most brutal on record, with the Donners attempting to cross snowdrifts ten to twenty feet high. It was nearly impossible for the group, with more than half of the remaining eighty-one people in the party under age eighteen. They settled in and waited out the winter as best they could. Before long, starvation set in, and members began dying in droves.

That's when the survivors of the Donner Party resorted to what would make them famous for the ages: cannibalism.

Flesh from the dead was cut off and meticulously labeled to prevent a survivor from having to eat their own family member. Georgia Donner, age four during the ordeal, later recalled being fed strange bits of meat: "Father was crying and did not look at us the entire time. . . . There was nothing else."

All of this, mind you, because they were tempted by a shortcut.

There's a scene in the movie *Lawrence of Arabia* in which Lawrence puts out a match with his fingers and doesn't flinch. Another man watching tries to do the same and yells in pain.

"It hurts! What's the trick, then?" he asks.

"The trick is not minding that it hurts," Lawrence says.

This is one of the most useful life skills—enduring the pain when necessary rather than assuming there's a hack, or a shortcut, around it.

A coworker of mine at an old employer once hired a social media consultant. During a three-hour session, the consultant walked us through hashtags, what time of day you should post on Twitter, how threading posts increases engagement, and a slew of other hacks.

He was nice. But he never mentioned the most effective social media trick: write good stuff that people want to read.

That's because writing good stuff isn't a hack. It's hard. It takes time and creativity. It can't be manufactured. It works, with a near 100 percent success rate. But it is the social media equivalent of a heavy workout.

Same goes for diets, finances, marketing . . . everyone wants a shortcut. It's always been this way, but I suspect it's getting worse as technology inflates our benchmark for how fast results should happen.

Hacks are appealing because they look like paths to prizes without the effort. But in the real world, those rarely exist.

Charlie Munger once noted: "The safest way to try to get what you want is to try to deserve what you want. It's such a simple idea. It's the golden rule. You want to deliver to the world what you would buy if you were on the other end."

In 1990, David Letterman asked his friend Jerry Seinfeld how his new sitcom was going.

Jerry said there was one frustrating problem: NBC supplied the show with teams of comedy writers, and he didn't think he was getting much good material from them.

"Wouldn't it be weirder if they were good?" David asked.

"What do you mean?" Jerry asked.

"Wouldn't it be strange if they could all just produce reams of hilarious material day after day?"

Recalling the conversation, Seinfeld laughed and told Letterman: "It's supposed to be hard."

Of course it is. The reason someone like Jerry Seinfeld, or Michael Jordan, or Serena Williams is so famous is because there is only one of them. What they've accomplished is unfathomably hard, and *that* is what we admire.

Harvard Business Review once pointed out to Jerry Seinfeld that part of the reason he ended his show was writer burnout. The magazine asked if he and show cocreator Larry David could have avoided burnout and kept the show going if they used a consulting company like McKinsey to create a more efficient writing process.

Seinfeld asked if McKinsey is funny.

No, the magazine said.

"Then I don't need them," he said. "If you're efficient, you're doing it the wrong way. The right way is the hard way. The show was successful because I micromanaged it—every word, every line, every take, every edit, every casting."

If you're efficient, you're doing it the wrong way.

That is so counterintuitive. But I think it perfectly highlights the danger of shortcuts.

Part of this is simply understanding the costs of success.

Jeff Bezos once talked about the realities of loving your job:

> If you can get your work life to where you enjoy half of it, that is amazing. Very few people ever achieve that.
>
> Because the truth is, everything comes with overhead. That's reality. Everything comes with pieces that you don't like.
>
> You can be a Supreme Court justice and there's still going to be pieces of your job you don't like. You can be a university professor and you still have to go to committee meetings. Every job comes with pieces you don't like.
>
> And we need to say: That's part of it.

That's part of it.

It's part of everything. His advice applies to so much more than careers.

A simple rule that's obvious but easy to ignore is that nothing worth pursuing is free. How could it be otherwise? Everything has a price, and the price is usually proportionate to the potential rewards.

But there's rarely a price tag. And you don't pay the price with cash. Most things worth pursuing charge their fee in the form of stress, uncertainty, dealing with quirky people, bureaucracy, other peoples' conflicting incentives, hassle, nonsense, long hours, and constant doubt. That's the overhead cost of getting ahead.

A lot of times that price is worth paying. But you have to realize that it's a price that must be paid. There are few coupons, and sales are rare.

———

A thing that's easy to overlook in life is that there is a certain level of inefficiency that is not only inevitable, but ideal.

Steven Pressfield wrote for thirty years before publishing *The Legend of Bagger Vance*. His career leading up to then was bleak; at one point he lived in a halfway house for the cheap rent.

He once described the people who lived there as the funniest and most interesting people he had ever met. He said he soon realized they weren't crazy at all. They were, instead, "the smartest people" who had just "seen through the bullshit." And because of that, "they couldn't function in the world."

"They couldn't hold a job because they just couldn't take the bullshit," he said. The rest of the world saw these people as rejects because they couldn't fit in. But in fact, Pressfield said, they were the geniuses who simply couldn't stand everyone else's nonsense.

This reminds me of something I've long believed.

If you recognize that inefficiency—"bullshit," as Pressfield puts it—is ubiquitous, then the question is not "How can I avoid all of it?" but "What is the optimal amount to put up with so I can still function in a messy and imperfect world?"

If your tolerance is zero—if you are allergic to differences in opinion, personal incentives, emotions, inefficiencies, miscommunication, and such—your odds of succeeding in anything that requires other people rounds to zero. You can't function in the world, as Pressfield says. The other end of the spectrum—fully accepting every incidence of nonsense and hassle—is just as bad. The world will eat you alive.

What's easy to miss is that there are bad things that become bigger problems when you try to eliminate them. I think the most successful people recognize when a certain amount of acceptance beats purity. Theft is a good example. A grocery store could eliminate theft by strip-searching every customer leaving the store. But then no one would shop there. So the optimal level of theft is never zero. You accept a certain level as an inevitable cost of progress.

Inefficiency, in all its forms, is similar.

A unique skill, an underrated skill, is identifying the optimal amount of hassle and nonsense you should put up with to get ahead while getting along.

Franklin Roosevelt—the most powerful man in the world, whose paralysis meant his aides often had to carry him to the bathroom—once said, "If you can't use your legs and they bring you milk when you wanted orange juice, you learn to say 'that's all right,' and drink it."

Every industry and career is different, but there's universal value in accepting hassle when reality demands it.

Volatility. People having bad days. Office politics. Difficult personalities. Bureaucracy. All of them are bad. But all have to be endured to some degree if you want to get anything done.

Many managers have little tolerance for nonsense. They think it's noble. *I demand excellence*, they say. But it's just unrealistic. The huge majority of them won't thrive in their careers. Compounding is fueled by endurance, so sitting through periods of insanity is not a defect; it's accepting an optimal level of hassle.

Same in business. My friend Brent says running a company is like eating glass while being punched in the face. "Often nothing works. Emotions run wild. Confusion reigns." He's also equated it to a daily battle—you wake up every morning, grab your knife, fight off challenges, and pray you make it home alive. But dealing with that hassle is the entire reason why it can be lucrative. "Where there's pain there's profit," he often reminds people. There's an optimal level of hassle to accept, even embrace.

Another upside: Once you accept a certain level of inefficiency, you stop denying its existence and have a clearer view of how the world works.

I was once on a flight with a CEO—he let everyone know that's what he was—who lost his mind after we had to change gates twice. I wondered: How did he make it this far in life without the ability to deal with petty annoyances outside of his control? The most likely answer is that he lives in denial over what he thinks he's in control of and demands unrealistic precision from subordinates who compensate by hiding bad news.

A good rule of thumb for a lot of things is to identify the price and be willing to pay it. The price, for so many things, is putting up with an optimal amount of hassle.

Next, a painful truth: The only thing harder than gaining a competitive advantage is keeping one.

Keep Running

**Most competitive advantages
eventually die.**

EVOLUTION IS GOOD at what it does. And one of the things
it does is give animals bigger bodies over time.

Edward Drinker Cope was a nineteenth-century paleontologist.
His work, later deemed Cope's Rule—not universal enough to call
a law—tracked the lineages of thousands of species and showed a
clear bias toward animals evolving to become larger over time.

Horses went from the size of small dogs to their modern height.
Snakes from no longer than an inch to modern boas. Dinosaurs
from three-inch lizards to a brontosaurus. And humans, from
ancestors who millions of years ago averaged less than four feet
in height as adults to our modern stature.

This isn't surprising. Bigger species are better at capturing prey,
can travel longer distances, and can support bigger brains.

The obvious question is: *Why hasn't evolution made every species
enormous?*

Two scientists, Aaron Clauset of the Santa Fe Institute and
Douglas Erwin of the Museum of Natural History, explained

why in a paper that summed it up in a wonderful sentence: "The tendency for evolution to create larger species is counterbalanced by the tendency of extinction to kill off larger species."

Body size in biology is like leverage in investing: It accentuates the gains but amplifies the losses. It works well for a while and then backfires spectacularly at the point where the benefits are nice but the losses are lethal.

Take injury. Big animals are fragile. An ant can fall from an elevation fifteen thousand times its height and walk away unharmed. A rat will break bones falling from an elevation fifty times its height. A human will die from a fall at ten times its height. An elephant falling from twice its height splashes like a water balloon.

Big animals also require lots of land per capita, which is brutal when land becomes scarce. They need more food per unit of body mass than small animals, which is the end game in a famine. They can't hide easily. They move slow. They reproduce slowly. Their top-of-the-food-chain status means they usually don't need to adapt, which is an unfortunate trait when adapting is required. The most dominant creatures tend to be huge, but the most enduring tend to be smaller. T-Rex < cockroach < bacteria.

What's incredible about this is that evolution encourages you to get bigger, then punishes you for being big.

It's a telling sign of what happens in so many areas of life: Competitive advantages don't stick around for long.

Let me show you how this played out in one of America's most storied companies: Sears.

The only thing harder than gaining a competitive edge is not losing an advantage when you have one.

If you were a movie scriptwriter and had to dream up a fake company with the strongest competitive advantage you can imagine, you would probably come up with something that looks like what Sears was in the 1970s.

Sears was the largest retailer in the world, housed in the tallest building in the world, employing one of the largest workforces.

"No one has to tell you you've come to the right place. The look of merchandising authority is complete and unmistakable," *The New York Times* wrote of Sears in 1983.

Sears was so good at retailing that in the 1970s and '80s it ventured into other areas, like finance. It owned Allstate Insurance, Discover credit card company, the Dean Witter brokerage for your stocks, and the Coldwell Banker brokerage for your house.

Sears was, in almost every way, the Amazon of its day: so dominant at retailing efficiency that it could spread its magic into unrelated industries, where it would terrify rivals. *The Times* wrote in 1974:

> Donald T. Regan, chairman of Merrill Lynch . . . indicated yesterday that the firm sees itself eventually as a Sears, Roebuck of the investment business. . . . "We must get as efficient as possible to keep costs to the consumer down," he said. "That's what made Sears a success, and that's a rule we must keep in mind."

And then everything fell to pieces.

Growing income inequality pushed consumers to either bargain or luxury goods, leaving Sears in the shrinking middle. Competition from Walmart and Target—younger and hungrier retailers—took off.

By the late 2000s, Sears was a shell of its former self. YES, WE ARE OPEN a sign outside my local Sears read—a reminder to customers who had all but written it off.

The story of how Sears lost its competitive advantage is fascinating. But it is not unique. It is in many ways the default outcome of once-dominant companies.

Going public is a sign that a company has found enough

competitive advantage to scale into a large corporation. But almost 40 percent of all public companies lost all their value from 1980 to 2014. The list of top ten Fortune 500 companies that went bankrupt includes General Motors, Chrysler, Kodak—and Sears. The list of those unrecognizable from their former selves is longer, and includes General Electric, Time Warner, AIG, and Motorola. Countries follow similar fates. At various points in the past, the world's scientific and economic progress has been dominated by Asia, Europe, and the Middle East.

Whenever a once powerful thing loses an advantage, it is tempting to ridicule the mistakes of its leaders. But it's easy to overlook how many forces pull you away from a competitive advantage once you have one, specifically *because* you have one. Success has its own gravity. "The higher the monkey climbs a tree, the more you can see his ass," oil tycoon T. Boone Pickens used to say.

Five big things tend to eat away at competitive advantages.

One is that being right instills confidence that you can't be wrong, which is a devastating characteristic in a world where outlier success has a target on its back, with competitors in tow. Size is associated with success, success is associated with hubris, and hubris is the beginning of the end of success.

Another is that success tends to lead to growth, usually by design, but a big organization is a different animal than a small one, and strategies that lead to success at one size can be impossible at another. There is a long history of star investment fund managers from one decade underperforming in the next. Some of this is the unraveling of luck. But success also attracts capital, and a big investment fund isn't as nimble as a small one. The career version of this is the Peter Principle: talented workers will keep getting promoted until they're in over their head, when they fail.

A third is the irony that people often work hard to gain a

competitive advantage for the intended purpose of not having to work so hard at some point in the future. Hard work is in pursuit of a goal, and once that goal is met the relaxation that feels so justified removes paranoia. This allows competitors and a changing world to creep in unnoticed.

A fourth is that a skill that's valuable in one era may not extend to the next. You can work as hard and be as paranoid as you've always been, but if the world no longer values your skill, it's a loss. Being a one-trick pony is common, because people and companies that are very good at one specific thing tend to be the highest paid during the boom.

The last is that some success is owed to being in the right place at the right time. The reversion to reality that unmasks good luck is often only obvious with hindsight, and is both humbling and tempting not to believe.

The idea that advantage has a shelf life is a fundamental part of growth. It doesn't have to be a tragedy—not all competitive advantages end like Sears. Great Britain lost the economic and military supremacy it held in the nineteenth century and remained a pretty nice place to live in the twentieth.

But competitive advantages tend to be short-lived, often because their success plants the seeds of their own decline.

Leigh Van Valen was a crazy-looking evolutionary biologist who came up with a theory so wild no academic journal would publish it. So he created his own journal and published it, and the idea eventually became accepted wisdom.

Those kinds of ideas—counterintuitive, but ultimately true— are the ones worth paying most attention to, because they're easiest to overlook.

For decades, scientists assumed that the longer a species had been around, the more likely it was to stick around, because age proved a strength that was likely to endure. Longevity was seen as both a trophy and a forecast.

In the early 1970s, Van Valen set out to prove that the conventional wisdom was right. But he couldn't. The data just didn't fit.

He began to wonder whether evolution was such a relentless and unforgiving force that long-lived species were just lucky. The data fit *that* theory better.

You'd think a new species discovering its niche would be fragile and susceptible to extinction—let's say a 10 percent chance of extinction in a given period—while an old species had proven its might, and has, say, a 0.01 percent chance of extinction.

But when Van Valen plotted extinctions by a species' age, the trend looked more like a straight line.

Some species survived a long time. But among groups of species, the probability of extinction was roughly the same whether it was ten thousand years old or ten million years old.

In a 1973 paper titled "A New Evolutionary Law," Van Valen wrote that "the probability of extinction of a taxon is effectively independent of its age."

If you take a thousand marbles and remove 2 percent of them each year, some marbles will remain in the jar after twenty years. But the odds of being picked out are the same every year (2 percent). Marbles don't get better at staying in the jar.

Species are the same. Some happen to live a long time, but the odds of surviving don't improve over time.

Van Valen argued that's the case mainly because competition isn't like a football game that ends with a winner who can then take a break. Competition never stops. A species that gains an advantage over a competitor instantly incentivizes the competitor to improve. It's an arms race.

Evolution is the study of advantages. Van Valen's idea is simply that there are no permanent advantages. Everyone is madly scrambling all the time, but no one gets so far ahead that they become extinction-proof.

Some things evolve but never actually become better adapted, because threats are always changing. Black rhinos survived for eight million years before being killed off by poachers. Lehman Brothers adapted and prospered for a hundred and fifty years years and thirty three recessions before it met its match in mortgage-backed securities. Poof, gone.

No one's ever safe. No one can ever rest.

Van Valen called it the Red Queen hypothesis of evolution. In *Alice in Wonderland*, Alice meets the Red Queen in a land where you have to run just to stay in place:

> However fast they went, they never seemed to pass anything.
> "I wonder if all the things move along with us?" thought poor puzzled Alice. And the Queen seemed to guess her thoughts, for she cried, "Faster! Don't try to talk! Keep running!"

"Keep running" just to stay in place is how evolution works.

And isn't this how most things in modern life work?

Business?

Products?

Careers?

Countries?

Relationships?

Yes to all of them.

Evolution is ruthless and unforgiving—it doesn't teach by showing you what works but by destroying what doesn't.

One takeaway is that you should never be surprised when something that dominates one era dies off in the next. It's one of the most common stories in history. Few companies, products, musicians, cities, or authors remain relevant for more than a few decades, tops. The ones that have (the Beatles, Levi's, Snickers, New York City) are rare exceptions.

Another takeaway is to keep running. No competitive advantage is so powerful that it can let you rest on your laurels—and in fact the ones that appear to do so tend to seed their own demise.

Now let me share why it's so hard to gauge how good our future might be.

The Wonders of the Future

It always feels like we're falling behind,
and it's easy to discount the potential
of new technology.

THERE'S A TYPICAL path of how people respond to what eventually becomes a world-changing new technology:

- I've never heard of it.
- I've heard of it but don't understand it.
- I understand it, but I don't see how it's useful.
- I see how it could be fun for rich people, but not me.
- I use it, but it's just a toy.
- It's becoming more useful for me.
- I use it all the time.
- I could not imagine life without it.
- Seriously, people lived without it?
- It's too powerful and needs to be regulated.

It happens over and over again. It's very difficult to envision what one small invention has the potential to become one day.

A common view through history is that past innovation was magnificent, but future innovation must be limited because we've picked all the low-hanging fruit.

On January 12, 1908, *The Washington Post* ran a full-page spread headlined "America's Thinking Men Forecast the Wonders of the Future."

Among the "thinking men" buried in the fine print was Thomas Edison.

Edison had already changed the world at this point; he was the Steve Jobs of his time.

The *Post* editors asked: "Is the age of invention passing?"

Edison answered: "Passing?" he repeated, in apparent astonishment that such a question should be asked. "Why, it hasn't started yet. That ought to answer your question. Do you want anything else?"

"You believe, then, that the next 50 years will see as great a mechanical and scientific development as the past half century?" the *Post* queried Edison.

"Greater. Much greater," he replied.

"Along what lines do you expect this development?" they asked him.

"Along all lines."

This wasn't blind optimism. Edison understood the process of scientific discovery. Big innovations don't come at once, but rather are built up slowly when several small innovations are combined over time. Edison wasn't a grand planner. He was a prolific tinkerer, combining parts in ways he didn't quite understand, confident that little discoveries along the way would be combined and leveraged into more meaningful inventions.

Edison, for example, did not invent the first light bulb; he just greatly improved upon what others had already built. In 1802—three quarters of a century before Edison's lightbulb—a British inventor named Humphry Davy created an electric light called an arc lamp, using charcoal rods as a filament. It worked like Edison's lightbulb, but it was impractically bright—you'd nearly go blind looking at it—and could stay lit only for a few moments before burning out, so it was rarely used. Edison's contribution was moderating the bulb's brightness and longevity. That was an enormous breakthrough. But it was built on the back of dozens of previous breakthroughs, none of which seemed meaningful in their own right.

That was why Edison was so optimistic about innovation. He explained:

> You can never tell what apparently small discovery will lead to. Somebody discovers something and immediately a host of experimenters and inventors are playing all the variations upon it.

He gave some examples:

> Take Faraday's experiments with copper disks. Looked like a scientific plaything, didn't it? Well, it eventually gave us the trolley car. Or take Crookes' tubes; looked like an academic discovery, but we got the X-ray from it. A whole host of experimenters are at work today; what great things their discoveries will lead to, no one can foretell.

"You're asking if the age of invention is over?" Edison asked. "Why, we don't know anything yet."

This, of course, is exactly what happened.

When the airplane came into practical use in the early 1900s, one of the first tasks was trying to foresee what benefits would come from it. A few obvious ones were mail delivery and sky racing.

No one predicted nuclear power plants. But they wouldn't have been possible without the plane.

Without the plane we wouldn't have had the aerial bomb. Without the aerial bomb we wouldn't have had the nuclear bomb. And without the nuclear bomb we wouldn't have discovered the peaceful use of nuclear power.

Same thing today. Google Maps, TurboTax, and Instagram wouldn't be possible without ARPANET, a 1960s Department of Defense project linking computers to manage Cold War secrets, which became the foundation for the internet. That's how you go from the threat of nuclear war to filing your taxes from your couch—a link that was unthinkable fifty years ago, but there it is.

Author Safi Bahcall notes that Polaroid film was discovered when sick dogs that were fed quinine to treat parasites showed an unusual type of crystal in their urine. Those crystals turned out to be the best polarizers ever discovered.

Who predicts that? Who sees that coming? Nobody. Absolutely nobody.

Facebook similarly began as a way for college students to share pictures of their drunk weekends, and within a decade it was the most powerful lever in global politics. Again, it's just impossible to connect those dots with foresight.

And that's why all innovation is hard to predict and easy to underestimate. The path from A to Z can be so complex and end up at such a strange point that it's nearly impossible to look at today's tools and extrapolate what they might become. Someone somewhere right now is inventing or discovering something that will utterly change the future. But you're probably not going to know about it for years. That's always how it works.

There's a theory in evolutionary biology called Fisher's

Fundamental Theorem of Natural Selection. It's the idea that variance equals strength, because the more diverse a population is, the more chances it has to come up with new traits that can be selected for. No one can know what traits will be useful; that's not how evolution works. But if you create a lot of traits, the useful one—whatever it is—will be in there somewhere.

It's the same thing with innovation. At any given moment it's easy to look around at what start-ups are building or what scientists are discovering and think that what we're working on is *maybe neat*—at best—but pales in comparison to what we did yesterday. Since we never know how multiple innovations will collide, the path of least resistance is to conclude that our best days are behind us while ignoring the potential of what we're working on.

One takeaway here is that it's easy to always feel like we're falling behind. In most eras it can feel like we haven't invented anything useful for ten or twenty years. But that's merely because it can take ten or twenty years for an innovation to become useful. When you realize that progress is made step-by-step, slowly over time, you realize that tiny little innovations that no one thinks much of are the seeds for what has the potential to compound into something great.

Dee Hock says, "A book is far more than what the author wrote; it is everything you can imagine and read into it as well." It's similar with new technology. The value of every new technology is not just what it can do; it's what someone else with a totally different skill set and point of view can eventually manipulate it into.

Another takeaway is that it's so easy to underestimate how two small things can compound into an enormous thing. Take the way Mother Nature works: A little cool air from the north is no big deal. A little warm breeze from the south is pleasant. But when they mix together over Missouri you get a tornado.

That's called emergent effects, and they can be wildly powerful. Same with new technology. One boring thing plus one boring thing can equal one world-changing thing in a way that's hard to fathom if you don't respect exponential growth. The same thing happens in careers, when someone with a few mediocre skills mixed together at the right time becomes multiple times more successful than someone who's an expert in one thing.

On January 12, 1908—the same day the *Post* ran their column with Edison—the first long-distance wireless message was sent in France.

No one could foresee the inventions it eventually seeded, including helping me write this book and send it to the publisher a hundred and fourteen years later.

Same as ever.

Now, let me tell you a story about how good people are at disguising how hard their lives are.

Harder Than It Looks and Not as Fun as It Seems

"The grass is always greener on the side that's fertilized with bullshit."

I N 1963, *Life* magazine asked James Baldwin where he gets his inspiration. Baldwin responded:

> You think your pain and your heartbreak are unprecedented in the history of the world, but then you read. It was books that taught me that the things that tormented me most were the very things that connected me with all the people who were alive, or who ever had been alive. An artist is a sort of emotional historian.

It's a wonderful observation. But I think what he's describing here is rare.

Most people do not disclose what torments them, what they're scared of, what they're insecure about, or whether or not they're actually happy. Rarely will they give you an honest account of their flaws and failures.

The window-dressed version of ourselves is by far the most common.

There's a saying—I don't know whose—that an expert is always from out of town. It's similar to the Bible verse that says no man is a prophet in his own country. That one has deeper meaning, but they both get across an important point: It's easiest to convince people that you're special if they don't know you well enough to see all the ways you're not.

Keep that in mind when comparing your career, business, and life to those of others.

Good advice that took me awhile to learn is that everything is sales. *Everything is sales.* This is usually framed as career advice—no matter what your role in a company is, your ultimate job is to help sales.

But it applies to so many things.

Everything is sales also means that everyone is trying to craft an image of who they are. The image helps them sell themselves to others. Some are more aggressive than others, but everyone plays the image game, even if only subconsciously. Since they're crafting the image, it's not a complete view. There's a filter. Skills are advertised, flaws are hidden.

A friend once complained to me about how inefficient his employer is. Processes are poor, communication is bad. He then said a competitor company was far better and had its act together. I asked him how he knew that—he's never worked there and has never been inside the company. Fair, he said. It just seems that way from the outside.

But almost everything looks better from the outside.

I guarantee workers at the competitor find flaws in the way

their company operates, because they know about their company what my friend knows about his: how the sausage is made. All the messy personalities and difficult decisions that you see only when you're inside, in the trenches. "All businesses are loosely functioning disasters," Brent Beshore says. But a business is like an iceberg; only a fraction is visible.

It's the same for people.

Instagram is full of beach vacation photos, not flight delay photos. Résumés highlight career wins but are silent on doubt and worry. Investing gurus and business titans are easy to elevate to mythical status because you don't know them well enough to witness times when their decision-making process was ordinary, if not awful.

Of course there's a spectrum. Some companies operate better than others, some people are more insightful than average. A few are extraordinary.

But it's always hard to know where anyone sits on that spectrum when they've carefully crafted an image of who they are. "The grass is always greener on the side that's fertilized with bullshit," the saying goes.

Occasionally a window into reality cracks open. Warren Buffett's biography *The Snowball* revealed that the most-admired person in the investing industry has at times had a miserable family life—partly his own doing, the collateral damage of a life where picking stocks was the highest priority.

Same for Bill and Melinda Gates, whose life looked fairy-tale charmed right up until the news of their nasty divorce. Elon Musk once broke down in tears when asked about the mental toll of Tesla's struggles. "This has really come at the expense of seeing my kids. And seeing friends."

I grew up with a chronic stutter. People who have known me for years tend to say "I never knew you had a problem" when I tell them about it. It's a well-meaning comment, but it actually highlights the issue. You didn't know I stutter because I didn't talk when I knew it would be difficult for me. You never know what struggles people are hiding. I've always wondered how many people I know are stutterers, but, like me, have kept it mostly hidden. And how many other issues are like that? Depression, anxiety, phobias . . . so many things can be disguised in a way that places a facade of normalcy over a person's internal struggles.

Back to the iceberg: What most of us see most of the time is a fraction of what has actually happened, or what's going on inside people's heads. And it's stripped of all the hard parts.

Most things are harder than they look and not as fun as they seem.

It leads to a few things:

When you are keenly aware of your own struggles but blind to those of others, it's easy to assume you're missing some skill or secret that others have. The more we describe successful people as having superhuman powers, the more everyone else looks at them and says, "I could never do that." Which is unfortunate, because more people would be willing to try if they knew that those they admire are probably normal people who played the odds right.

When someone is viewed as more extraordinary than they are, you're more likely to overvalue their opinion on things they have no special talent in. Like a successful hedge fund manager's political views, or a politician's investment advice. Only when you get to know someone well do you realize the best you can do in life is to become an expert at some things while remaining inept at others—and that's if you're good. There's an important difference between someone whose specific talent should be celebrated versus someone whose ideas should never be questioned. Eat the orange, throw away the peel.

Everyone's dealing with problems they don't advertise, at least until you get to know them well. Keep that in mind and you become more forgiving—of yourself and others.

Next, an explanation of why good people do terrible things.

Incentives: The Most Powerful Force in the World

When the incentives are crazy, the behavior
is crazy. People can be led to justify and
defend nearly anything.

J ASON ZWEIG OF *The Wall Street Journal* says there are three
ways to be a professional writer:

1. Lie to people who want to be lied to, and you'll get rich.
2. Tell the truth to those who want the truth, and you'll make
    a living.
3. Tell the truth to those who want to be lied to, and you'll go
    broke.

What a wonderful summary of the power of incentives, and an explanation for why people do some of the crazy things they do.

———————

By age thirty-five, Akinola Bolaji had already spent two decades scamming people online, posing as an American fisherman to con vulnerable widows into sending him money.

The New York Times asked the Nigerian how he felt about causing so much harm to innocent people. He replied: "Definitely there is always conscience. But poverty will not make you feel the pain."

Scamming people is easier to justify in your head when you're starving.

Rapper Notorious B.I.G. once casually mentioned that he began selling crack in fourth grade.

He explained how it happened: Early on in life he was always interested in art. His teachers pushed him to become an artist and told him that he could actually make a living drawing. He began dreaming of becoming a commercial artist, designing billboards.

Then, one day, he got introduced to selling crack. He recalled: "Haha, now I'm thinking, commercial art?! Haha. I'm out here for twenty minutes and I can make some real, real money, man."

Soviet poet Yevgeny Yevtushenko once speculated that during Galileo's day, several scientists believed Earth revolved around the sun. "But they had families to feed," so they never spoke up.

These are extreme examples of something everyone—you, me, everyone—is susceptible to and more influenced by than we want to admit: Incentives are the most powerful force in the world and can get people to justify or defend almost anything.

When you understand how powerful incentives can be, you stop being surprised when the world lurches from one absurdity to the next. If asked, "How many people in the world are truly crazy?" I might say, I don't know, 3 percent to 5 percent. But if I asked, "How many people in the world would be willing to do something crazy if their incentives were right?" I'd say, oh, easily 50 percent or more.

No matter how much information and context you have, nothing is more persuasive than what you desperately want or need to be true. And as Daniel Kahneman once wrote, "It is easier to recognize other people's mistakes than our own." What makes incentives powerful is not just how they influence other people's decisions but how blind we can be to how they impact our own.

Ben Franklin once wrote, "If you would persuade, appeal to interest and not to reason." Incentives fuel stories that justify people's actions and beliefs, offering comfort even when they're doing things they know are wrong and believe things they know aren't true.

James Clear put it this way: "People follow incentives, not advice."

True story about a guy I knew well: A pizza delivery man who became a subprime mortgage banker in 2005.

Virtually overnight he could earn more per day than he earned per month delivering pizza. It completely changed his life.

Put yourself in his shoes. His job was to make loans. Feeding his family relied on making loans. And if he didn't make those loans someone else would, so protesting or quitting felt pointless.

Everyone knew the subprime mortgage game was a joke in the mid-2000s. Everyone knew it would end one day. But the bar for someone like my friend to say "This is unsustainable so I'm going to quit and deliver pizza again" is unbelievably high. It would be high for most of us. I didn't blame him then, and I don't blame him now.

A lot of bankers screwed up during the 2008 financial crisis. But too many of us underestimate how we ourselves would have acted if someone dangled enormous rewards in our face. Most people are blind to their own faults. To paraphrase Ben Franklin: Vice knows it's ugly, so it hides behind a mask.

This goes up the food chain, from the broker to the CEO, the investors, the real estate appraiser, the realtor, the house flipper, the politician, the central banker—incentives lean heavily toward not rocking the boat. So everyone keeps paddling long after the market becomes unsustainable.

Sometimes the behaviors and outcomes are more extreme.

A documentary on the former Mexican drug lord El Chapo shows the poor village in Mexico where the violent, murderous cartel leader was *extremely* popular and supported by locals. They would do anything to protect him. One of them explained:

> You're talking about people who have almost no income. It was not uncommon for El Chapo to stop and talk to someone and say, "What's going on in your life?" And the person would say, "Oh, my daughter is getting married." Chapo would say, "I'll take care of it." He'd get a big place, provide the band, provide the booze and food, and the whole town is invited. The father of the bride says, "Chapo made this possible."

In all these situations you have good, honest, well-meaning people who end up supporting or partaking in bad behavior because the incentives to play along are so strong. And in each situation there are more than just financial incentives. Incentives can be cultural and tribal, where people support things because they don't want to upset or become banished from their social group. A lot of people can resist financial incentives; cultural and tribal incentives are more seductive.

One of the strongest pulls of incentives is the desire for people to hear only what they want to hear and see only what they want to see.

In 1997 a religious cult called Heaven's Gate believed a spaceship traveling behind a comet was heading to Earth to pick up true believers and carry them to paradise.

Several cult members pitched in to buy a high-powered telescope. They wanted to see the spaceship with their own eyes.

They found the comet in the sky. But there was no spaceship following it.

So they took the telescope back to the store for a refund. The store manager asked if there was something wrong. They said yes, the telescope was clearly broken—because it didn't show the spaceship.

There's a long history of people believing what they want to believe.

And not just cult members.

It's just so hard to be purely objective when incentives push you toward one direction.

In 1923, Henry Luce wanted to create a magazine called *Facts*. It was going to report only on things that were objectively true. But Luce soon realized that was harder than you'd think. Instead he called it *Time*, with the idea that saving readers time with succinct stories was the most value a publisher could add. "Show me a man who thinks he's objective and I'll show you a man who's deceiving himself," Luce said.

Some variation of this applies to many fields, especially service industries where someone pays for an expert's opinion. There can be a difference between knowing what's right and making a living delivering what you know to be right.

This may be most common in investing, law, and medicine, when "do nothing" is the best answer, but "do something" is the career incentive.

Sometimes it's amoral, but it can be an innocent form of "cover your butt." Mostly, though, I think an advisor just feels useless if they tell a client "we don't need to do anything here." In the quest to be helpful they add complexity even when none is needed, or when it might backfire.

Years ago Jon Stewart interviewed investor and CNBC host Jim Cramer. When pressed on CNBC content that ranged from contradictory to inane, Cramer said, "Look, we've got seventeen hours of live TV a day to do." Stewart responded, "Maybe you can cut down on that." He's right. But if you're in the TV business, you can't.

A doctor once told me the biggest thing they don't teach in medical school is the difference between medicine and being a doctor—medicine is a biological science, while being a doctor is often a social skill of managing expectations, understanding the insurance system, communicating effectively, and so on.

Three things stick out here.

When good and honest people can be incentivized into crazy behavior, it's easy to underestimate the odds of the world going off the rails.

Everything from wars to recessions to frauds to business failures to market bubbles happen more often than people think because the moral boundaries of what people are willing to do can be extended with certain incentives.

That goes both ways. It's easy to underestimate how much good people can do, how talented they can become, and what they can accomplish when they operate in a world where their incentives are aligned toward progress.

Extremes are the norm.

Unsustainable things can last longer
than you anticipate.

Incentives can keep crazy, unsustainable trends going longer than seems reasonable because there are social and financial reasons preventing people from accepting reality for as long as they can.

A good question to ask is, "Which of my current views would change if my incentives were different?"

If you answer "none," you are likely not only persuaded but blinded by your incentives.

———————

Speaking of persuasion, let's discuss a related point: Nothing is more persuasive than what you've experienced firsthand.

Now You
Get It

**Nothing is more persuasive than what
you've experienced firsthand.**

NOTHING IS MORE persuasive than what you've experienced
firsthand. You can read and study and have empathy. But
you often have no clue what you're willing to do, what you want,
and how far you're willing to go until you've seen something with
your own eyes.

Harry Truman once said:

> The next generation never learns anything from the previous
> one until it's brought home with a hammer. . . . I've wondered
> why the next generation can't profit from the generation
> before, but they never do until they get knocked in the head
> by experience.

A big theme throughout history is that preferences are fickle, and people have no idea how they'll respond to an extreme shift in circumstance until they experience it for themselves.

———————

One of the most fascinating parts of the Great Depression isn't just that the economy collapsed, but how quickly and dramatically people's views changed as a result.

Americans voted Herbert Hoover into office in 1928 with one of the biggest landslides in history (444 electoral college votes). They voted him out in 1932 with a landslide in the other direction (59 electoral college votes).

Then the big changes began.

The gold standard, gone. Gold actually became illegal to own.

Public works surged.

Attempts to provide taxpayer-funded old-age pension insurance made no progress for decades, with supporters arrested on the Capitol lawn during the most serious push, after World War I. The Depression practically flipped a switch: a fringe idea was suddenly embraced. The Social Security Act was passed in 1935, 372–33 in the House of Representatives and 77–6 in the Senate.

On the other side of this was an alleged coup by wealthy businessmen to overthrow Franklin Roosevelt, with a Marine general named Smedley Butler taking his place as dictator, similar to fascist actions sweeping Europe at the time.

These are not the kind of things that occur when people have full stomachs and stable jobs. It's not until your life is upended, your hopes dashed, your dreams uncertain that people say, "What was that wild idea we heard before? Maybe we should give it a shot. Nothing else is working, might as well try."

Comedian Trevor Noah once discussed apartheid in his native South Africa, noting: "If you find the right balance between desperation and fear, you can make people do anything."

It's just so hard to understand that, and understand how you'll respond to risk, fear, and desperation, until you're in the heat of the moment.

Nowhere was this more powerful than in 1930s Germany, where the Great Depression was preceded by devastating hyperinflation that destroyed all paper wealth.

The book *What We Knew* features interviews with German civilians after World War II, seeking to understand how one of the most advanced and civilized cultures turned so sharp, so quickly, and committed the worst atrocities in human history:

> [Interviewer]: At the beginning of this interview, you said that most grown-ups welcomed Hitler's measures.
>
> [German civilian]: Yes, clearly. One has to remember that in 1923 we had the inflation. . . . The [currency] had inflated a trillion times. . . . Then Adolf came to power with his new idea. For most that was indeed better. People who hadn't had a job for years had a job. And then the people were all for the system.
>
> When someone helps you get out of an emergency situation and into a better life, then you're going to give them your support. Do you think people would then say, "This is all such nonsense. I'm against that"? No. That doesn't happen.

Or take Varlam Shalamov, a poet who spent fifteen years imprisoned in a gulag. He once wrote how quickly normal people can crack under stress and uncertainty. Take a good, honest, loving person and strip them of basic necessities and you'll soon get an unrecognizable monster who'll do anything to survive. Under high stress, "a man becomes a beast in three weeks," Shalamov wrote.

Historian Stephen Ambrose chronicled World War II soldiers who left basic training full of bravado and confidence, eager to fight when they joined the front lines. Then they get shot at, and everything changes.

"There was no way training could prepare a man for combat," Ambrose wrote. It could teach you how to fire a gun and follow orders. But "it could not teach men how to lie helpless under a shower of shrapnel in a field crisscrossed by machine-gun fire." No one could understand it until they experienced it.

These are some of the most extreme examples that exist. But the idea that people who are under stress quickly embrace ideas and goals they never would otherwise has left its fingerprints all over history.

Take 94 percent tax rates after World War II. Low taxes were the most popular economic platform of the 1920s, and anyone suggesting a hike was pushed aside. Then everything broke with the doubleheader Depression and war. In 1943 Franklin Roosevelt effectively capped incomes at the equivalent of $400,000 per year, with everything above that taxed at 94 percent. He was reelected in a landslide the next year.

Same with the Reagan revolution. Almost 80 percent of Americans had high trust in the government in 1964. Then the 1970s happened. Years of high inflation and high unemployment meant Americans were ready to listen to a politician who said the government was the cause of their problems, not the solution.

The big takeaway here is that we really have no idea what policies we'll be pushing for in, say, five or ten years. Unexpected hardship makes people do and think things they'd never imagine when things are calm.

Your personal views fall into the same trap. In investing, saying "I will be greedy when others are fearful" is easier said than done, because people underestimate how much their views and goals can change when markets break.

The reason you may embrace ideas and goals you once thought unthinkable during a downturn is because more changes during downturns than just asset prices.

If I, today, imagine how I'd respond to stocks falling 30 percent,

I picture a world where everything is like it is today *except* stock valuations, which are 30 percent cheaper.

But that's not how the world works.

Downturns don't happen in isolation. The reason stocks might fall 30 percent is because big groups of people, companies, and politicians screwed something up, and their screwups might sap my confidence in our ability to recover. So my investment priorities might shift from growth to preservation. It's difficult to contextualize this mental shift when the economy is booming. And even though Warren Buffett says to be greedy when others are fearful, far more people agree with that quote than actually act on it.

The same idea holds true for companies, careers, and relationships. Hard times make people do and think things they'd never imagine when things are calm.

Chris Rock once joked about who actually teaches kids in school: "Teachers do one half, bullies do the other," he said. "And learning how to deal with bullies is the half you'll actually use as a grown-up." It's real experience with risk and uncertainty, which is something you cannot fathom until you've experienced it firsthand.

Keep in mind, this works both ways. People often have no idea how they'll respond to a big windfall or an incredible gift of good luck until they've experienced it firsthand.

Going to the moon is the coolest thing humans have ever done.

You'd think it would be an overwhelming experience. But as the spacecraft hovered over the moon, Michael Collins turned to Neil Armstrong and Buzz Aldrin and said:

> It's amazing how quickly you adapt. It doesn't seem weird at all
> to me to look out there and see the moon going by, you know?

Three months later, after Al Bean walked on the moon during Apollo 12, he turned to astronaut Pete Conrad and said, "It's kind of like the song: Is that all there is?" Conrad was relieved, because he secretly felt the same, describing his moonwalk as spectacular but not momentous.

Expectations also shift and goalposts move faster than you can imagine. Collins once said of Aldrin: "I think he resents not being first on the moon more than he appreciates being second."

I don't think I've met, or know of, anyone with outsize success who gained as much happiness as an outsider might expect. That doesn't mean success can't bring pride or contentment or independence. But it's rarely what you thought it would be before achieving it.

Jim Carrey once said, "I think everybody should get rich and famous and do everything they ever dreamed of so they can see that it's not the answer."

Part of this is the same reason that predicting how you'll respond to risk is difficult: It's hard to imagine the full context until you experience it firsthand.

If you think of your future self living in a new mansion, you imagine basking in splendor and everything feeling great. What's easy to forget is that people in mansions can get the flu, have psoriasis, become embroiled in lawsuits, bicker with their spouses, feel wracked with insecurity and annoyed with politicians—which in any given moment can supersede any joy that comes from material success. Future fortunes are imagined in a vacuum, but reality is always lived with the good and bad taken together, competing for attention.

You might think you know how it'll feel. Then you experience it firsthand and you realize, ah, okay. It's more complicated than you thought.

Now you get it.

Next, let's talk about the long run.

Time
Horizons

Saying "I'm in it for the long run" is a bit
like standing at the base of Mount Everest,
pointing to the top, and saying, "That's
where I'm heading." Well, that's nice.
Now comes the test.

Nothing will ever separate us.
We will probably be married another ten years.

—*Elizabeth Taylor, five days before filing for divorce*

L ONG-TERM THINKING IS easier to believe in than to
accomplish.

Most people know it's the right strategy in investing, careers,
relationships—anything that compounds. But saying "I'm in it for
the long run" is a bit like standing at the base of Mount Everest,

pointing to the top, and saying, "That's where I'm heading." Well, that's nice. Now comes the test.

Long term is harder than most people imagine, which is why it's more lucrative than many people assume.

Everything worthwhile has a price, and the prices aren't always obvious. The real price of long term—the skills required, the mentality needed—is easy to minimize and often summarized with simple phrases like "Be more patient," as if that explains why so many people can't.

To do long term effectively you have to understand a few points.

The long run is just a collection of short runs you have to put up with.

Saying you have a ten-year time horizon doesn't exempt you from all the nonsense that happens in the next ten years. Everyone has to experience the recessions, the bear markets, the meltdowns, the surprises, and the memes.

So rather than assuming long-term thinkers don't have to deal with short-term nonsense, ask the question, "How can I endure a never-ending parade of nonsense?"

Long-term thinking can be a deceptive safety blanket that people assume lets them bypass the painful and unpredictable short run. But it never does. It might be the opposite: The longer your time horizon, the more calamities and disasters you'll experience. Baseball player Dan Quisenberry once said, "The future is much like the present, only longer."

Dealing with that reality requires a certain kind of alignment that's easy to overlook.

Your belief in the long run isn't enough. Your partners, coworkers, spouses, and friends have to sign up for the ride.

An investment manager who loses 40 percent can tell his investors, "It's okay, we're in this for the long run" and believe it. But the investors may not believe it. They might bail. The firm might not survive. Then even if the manager turns out to be right, it doesn't matter—no one's around to benefit.

The same thing happens when you have the guts to stick it out but your spouse doesn't.

Or when you have a great idea that will take time to prove, but your boss and coworkers aren't as patient.

These are not rarities. They're some of the most common outcomes in life.

A lot of it comes from the gap between what you believe and what you can convince other people of.

People mock how much short-term thinking there is in the financial industry, and they should. But I also get it: The reason so many financial professionals stray toward short-termism is because it's the only way to run a viable business when customers flee at the first sign of trouble. But the reason customers flee is often because investors have done such a poor job communicating how investing works, what their strategy is, what they should expect as an investor, and how to deal with inevitable volatility and cyclicality.

Eventually being right is one thing. But can you eventually be right *and* convince those around you? That's completely different, and easy to overlook.

Patience is often stubbornness in disguise.

The world changes, which makes changing your mind not just helpful, but crucial.

But changing your mind is hard because fooling yourself into believing a falsehood is so much easier than admitting a mistake.

Long-term thinking can become a crutch for those who are wrong but don't want to change their mind. They say, "I'm just early" or "Everyone else is crazy" when they can't let go of something that used to be true but the world has moved on from.

Doing long-term thinking well requires identifying when you're being patient versus just stubborn. Not an easy thing to do. The only solution is knowing the very few things in your industry that will never change and putting everything else in a bucket that's in constant need of updating and adapting. The few (very few) things that never change are candidates for long-term thinking. Everything else has a shelf life.

Long term is less about time horizon and more about flexibility.

If it's 2010 and you say "I have a ten-year time horizon," your target date is 2020. Which is when the world fell to pieces. If you were a business or an investor it was a terrible time to assume the world was ready to hand you the reward you had been patiently awaiting.

A long time horizon with a firm end date can be as reliant on chance as a short time horizon.

Far superior is flexibility.

Time is compounding's magic, and its importance can't be minimized. But the odds of success fall deepest in your favor when you mix a long time horizon with a flexible end date—or an indefinite horizon.

Benjamin Graham said, "The purpose of the margin of safety is to render the forecast unnecessary." The more flexibility you have, the less you need to know what happens next.

And never forget John Maynard Keynes: "In the long run we're all dead."

———————

Another point about long-term thinking is how it sways the information we consume.

I try to ask when I'm reading: Will I care about this a year from now? Ten years from now? Eighty years from now?

It's fine if the answer is no, even a lot of the time. But if you're honest with yourself you may begin to steer toward the more enduring bits of information.

There are two types of information: permanent and expiring.

Permanent information is: "How do people behave when they encounter a risk they hadn't fathomed?" Expiring information is: "How much profit did Microsoft earn in the second quarter of 2005?"

Expiring knowledge catches more attention than it should, for two reasons.

One, there's a lot of it, eager to keep our short attention spans occupied.

Two, we chase it down, anxious to squeeze insight out of it before it loses relevance.

Permanent information is harder to notice because it's buried in books rather than blasted in headlines. But its benefit is huge. It's not just that permanent information never expires, letting you accumulate it. It also compounds over time, leveraging off what you've already learned. Expiring information tells you what happened; permanent information tells you why something happened and is likely to happen again. That "why" can translate and interact with stuff you know about other topics, which is where the compounding comes in.

I read newspapers and books every day. I cannot recall one damn thing I read in a newspaper from, say, 2011. But I can tell you in detail about a few great books I read in 2011 and how they changed the way I think. I'll remember them forever. I'll keep reading newspapers. But if I read more books I'd probably develop better filters and frameworks that would help me make better sense of the news.

The point, then, isn't that you should read less news and more books. It's that if you read good books you'll have an easier time understanding what you should or shouldn't pay attention to in the news.

Next up: When trying too hard backfires.

Trying Too Hard

There are no points awarded
for difficulty.

LET'S DISCUSS AN enduring quirk of human behavior: the allure of complexity, intellectual stimulation, and discounting things that are simple but very effective, in preference to things that are complex but less effective.

In 2013 Harold Varmus, then director of the National Cancer Institute, gave a speech describing how difficult the war on cancer had become. Eradicating cancer—the National Cancer Act's goal when it was signed in 1971—seemed perpetually distant. Varmus said:

> There's a paradox that we must now honestly confront. Despite the extraordinary progress we've made in understanding the

underlying defects in cancer cells, we have not succeeded in controlling cancer as a human disease to the extent that I believe is possible.

One of the missing pieces, he said, is that we focus too much on cancer treatment and not enough on cancer prevention. If you wanted to get the next big leg up in the war on cancer, you had to make prevention the front line.

But prevention is boring, especially compared to the science and prestige of cancer treatments. So even if we know how important it is, it's hard for smart people to take it seriously.

MIT cancer researcher Robert Weinberg once described it this way: You can't die from cancer if you don't get cancer in the first place. But that simple truth is easy to overlook, because it's not intellectually stimulating.

> Persuading somebody to quit smoking is a psychological exercise. It has nothing to do with molecules and genes and cells. And so people like me are essentially uninterested in it.

That's in spite of the fact, he says, that getting people to quit smoking can make a bigger impact in the war on cancer than anything he, as a biologist, can do in his lifetime.

It's astounding, isn't it?

Here you have one of the top cancer researchers in the world, and he's saying he could make a bigger impact on cancer if he focused on getting people to quit smoking—but that's not *intellectually stimulating* enough for him. Or for many scientists, for that matter.

Now, I don't blame him—and Weinberg has added enormous value to the war on cancer.

But here we have an example of complexity being favored for its excitement, when simplicity may actually do a better job.

And that, I'll tell you, is a big lesson that applies to many things.

Computer scientist Edsger Dijkstra once wrote:

> Simplicity is the hallmark of truth—we should know better,
> but complexity continues to have a morbid attraction. When
> you give an academic audience a lecture that is crystal clear
> from alpha to omega, your audience feels cheated. . . . The sore
> truth is that complexity sells better.

The sore truth is that complexity sells better.

Of course it does. We see that everywhere.

To take a simple example: The U.S. Constitution is 7,591 words. Compare that to the average mortgage contract, which is over 15,000 words, and Apple's iCloud terms of service agreement, which is 7,314 words. The U.S. tax code is over 11 million words.

Sometimes length is necessary. When the Allies met to discuss what to do with Germany after World War II, Winston Churchill noted, "We are dealing with the fate of eighty million people and that requires more than eighty minutes to consider."

But in most situations a handful of simple variables drives the majority of outcomes. If you've covered the few things that matter, you're all set. A lot of what gets added after that is unnecessary filler that is either intellectually seductive, wastes your time, or is designed to confuse or impress you.

Nature has figured this out.

Samuel Williston was a nineteenth-century paleontologist who first noticed a historic trend in the reduction of body parts. Primitive animals often had many duplicate body parts, then evolution reduced the number but increased their usefulness. "The course of evolution has been to reduce the number of parts and to adapt those which remain more closely with their special uses, either by increase in size or by modifications of their shape and structure," Williston wrote in 1914.

Animals with hundreds of teeth often evolved to have a handful of specialized incisors, canines, and molars. Dozens of jawbones fused into two big ones. Skulls often made up of hundreds of tiny bones evolved into typically fewer than thirty.

Evolution figured out its version of simplification. It (if you can imagine evolution talking) says, "Get all that useless crap out of the way. Just give me the few things I need and make them effective."

A trick to learning a complicated topic is realizing how many complex details are cousins of something simple. John Reed wrote in his book *Succeeding*:

> When you first start to study a field, it seems like you have
> to memorize a zillion things. You don't. What you need is
> to identify the core principles—generally three to twelve of
> them—that govern the field. The million things you thought
> you had to memorize are simply various combinations of the
> core principles.

This is so vital. In finance, spending less than you make, saving the difference, and being patient is perhaps 90 percent of what you need to know to do well. But what's taught in college? How to price derivatives and calculate net present value. In health it's sleep eight hours, move a lot, eat real food, but not too much. But what's popular? Supplements, hacks, and pills.

Mark Twain said kids provide the most interesting information, "for they tell all they know and then they stop." Adults tend to lose this skill. Or they learn a new skill: how to dazzle with nonsense. Stephen King explains in his book *On Writing*:

This is a short book because most books about writing are filled with bullshit. I figured the shorter the book, the less bullshit.

Poetry.

———————

The question then is: Why? Why are complexity and length so appealing when simplicity and brevity will do?

A few reasons:

Complexity gives a comforting impression of control, while simplicity is hard to distinguish from cluelessness.

In most fields a handful of variables dictate the majority of outcomes. But paying attention to only those few variables can feel like you're leaving too much of the outcome to fate. The more knobs you can fiddle with—the hundred-tab spreadsheet, or the Big Data analysis—the more control you feel you have over the situation, if only because the impression of knowledge increases.

The flip side is that paying attention to only a few variables while ignoring the majority of others can make you look ignorant. If a client says, "What about this, what's happening here?" and you respond, "Oh, I have no idea, I don't even look at that," the odds that you'll sound uninformed are greater than the odds you'll sound like you've mastered simplicity.

Things you don't understand create a mystique around people who do.

If you say something I didn't know but can understand, I might think you're smart. If you say something I can't understand,

I might think you have an ability to think about a topic in ways I can't, which is a whole different species of admiration. When you understand things I don't, I have a hard time judging the limits of your knowledge in that field, which makes me more prone to taking your views at face value.

Length is often the only thing that can signal effort and thoughtfulness.

A typical nonfiction book covering a single topic is perhaps 250 pages, or something like 65,000 words.

The funny thing is the average reader does not come close to finishing most books they buy. Even among bestsellers, average readers quit after a few dozen pages. Length, then, has to serve a purpose other than providing more material.

My theory is that length indicates the author has spent more time thinking about a topic than you have, which can be the only data point signaling they might have insights you don't. It doesn't mean their thinking is right. And you may understand their point after two chapters. But the purpose of chapters 3–16 is often to show that the author has done so much work that chapters 1 and 2 might have some insight. Same goes for research reports and white papers.

Simplicity feels like an easy walk. Complexity feels like a mental marathon.

If the reps don't hurt when you're exercising, you're not really exercising. Pain is the sign of progress that tells you you're paying the unavoidable cost of admission. Short and simple communication is different. Richard Feynman and Stephen Hawking could teach math with simple language that didn't hurt your head, not because they dumbed down the topics but because they knew how to get from A to Z in as few steps as possible. An effective rule of thumb doesn't bypass complexity; it wraps things you don't understand into things you do. Like a baseball player who—by keeping a ball level in his gaze—knows where the ball will land as well as a physicist calculating the ball's flight with precision.

The problem with simplicity is that the reps don't hurt, so you don't feel like you're getting a mental workout. It can create a preference for laborious learning that students are actually okay with because it feels like a cognitive bench press, with all the assumed benefits.

———

Thomas McCrae was a young nineteenth-century doctor still unsure of his skills. One day he diagnosed a patient with a common, insignificant stomach ailment. McCrae's medical school professor watched the diagnosis and interrupted with every student's nightmare: in fact, the patient had a rare and serious disease. McCrae had never heard of it.

The diagnosis required immediate surgery. After opening the patient up, the professor realized that McCrae's initial diagnosis was correct. The patient was fine.

McCrae later wrote that he actually felt fortunate for never having heard of the rare disease.

It allowed his mind to settle on the most likely diagnosis, rather than be burdened by searching for rare diseases, like his more educated professor.

He wrote: "The moral of this is not that ignorance is an advantage. But some of us are too much attracted by the thought of rare things and forget the law of averages in diagnosis."

That idea is not intuitive, so it can drive you crazy. And it's hard to pinpoint when it occurs—maybe McCrae's professor was being appropriately cautious?

But a truth that applies to almost every field is that there are no points awarded for difficulty. It's possible to try too hard, to be too attracted to complexity, and doing so can backfire spectacularly.

We've made it to the last chapter. It's one of my favorites.

Wounds Heal,
Scars Last

What have you experienced that I haven't
that makes you believe what you do? And
would I think about the world like you do
if I experienced what you have?

DRIVE PAST THE PENTAGON, in Washington, D.C., and
there is no trace of the plane that crashed into its walls on
September 11, 2001.

But drive three minutes down the road, to Reagan National
Airport, and the scars of 9/11 are everywhere. Shoes off, jackets
off, belts off, toothpaste out, hands up, and empty your water
bottle while going through security.

Here's a common theme in the way people think: Wounds
heal, but scars last.

There's a long history of people adapting and rebuilding while
the scars of their ordeal remain forever, changing how they think
about risk, reward, opportunities, and goals for as long as they live.

An important component of human behavior is that people who've had different experiences than you will think differently than you do. They'll have different goals, outlooks, wishes, and values. So most debates are not actual disagreements; they're people with different experiences talking over each other.

Let me share a few times in history when the weight of personal experiences led to massive shifts in people's outlook on life.

More than thirty million people—about the population of California—died over four years on the eastern front during World War II. The dozen or so territories that made up the Soviet Republic represented about 10 percent of the world's population in 1940. By 1945, nearly 14 percent of that group was dead. Seventy *thousand* villages were completely destroyed.

There are stories of people still finding bones, bullets, and bombs in this region today, but most of the physical damage of the war was cleaned up by 1960. Industries rebuilt. People reorganized. Total population surpassed its prewar level less than a decade after the war ended.

This trend was more noticeable in Japan, whose economy opened up to global markets after the war. In 1946 Japan was producing enough food to provide only 1,500 calories a day for its people. By 1960 it was one of the fastest-growing economies in the world. Its GDP increased from $91 billion in 1965 to $1.1 trillion in 1980, with technology and manufacturing rivaling and surpassing any other region in the world.

The same is true for recessions—things heal. And markets—things recover. And businesses—past mistakes are forgotten.

But scars last.

A study of twenty thousand people from thirteen countries who lived through World War II found they were 3 percent more likely to have diabetes as adults and 6 percent more likely to suffer depression. Compared to those who avoided the war, they were less likely to marry and less satisfied with their lives as older adults.

In 1952, Frederick Lewis Allen wrote about those who lived through the Great Depression:

> [They] were gnawed at by a constant lurking fear of worse things yet, and in all too many cases actually went hungry. . . .
>
> [They cast] a cynical eye upon the old Horatio Alger formula for success; to be dubious about taking chances for ambition's sake; to look with a favorable eye upon a safe if unadventurous job, social insurance plans, pension plans. They had learned from bitter experience to crave security.

They had learned from bitter experience to crave security.

This, again, was written in the 1950s, when the U.S. economy was roaring and the unemployment rate was near a record low of less than 3 percent.

It is too easy to examine history and say, "Look, if you just held on and took a long-term view, things recovered and life went on," without realizing that mindsets are harder to repair than buildings and cash flows.

We can see and measure just about everything in the world except people's moods, fears, hopes, grudges, goals, triggers, and expectations. That's partly why history is such a continuous chain of baffling events, and always will be.

———————

Psychologist Ivan Pavlov trained his dogs to drool.

He did this by ringing a bell before they were fed. The dogs learned to associate the sound of the bell with an imminent meal, which triggered a salivary response.

Pavlov's dogs became famous for teaching psychologists about the science of learned behavior.

Less known is what happened to the poor dogs years later.

A massive flood in 1924 swept through Leningrad, where Pavlov kept his lab and kennel. Flood water came right up to the dogs' cages. Several were killed. The surviving dogs were forced to swim a quarter mile to safety. Pavlov later called it the most traumatic thing the dogs had ever experienced, by far.

Something fascinating then happened: The dogs seemingly forgot their learned behavior of drooling when the bell rang.

Pavlov wrote about one dog eleven days after the floodwaters receded:

> After the application of the [bell] all the remaining conditioned reflexes almost completely disappeared, the animal again declined the food, became very restless and continuously stared at the door.

Ever the curious scientist, Pavlov spent months studying how the flood changed his dogs' behavior. Many were never the same—they had completely different personalities after the flood, and learned behavior that was previously ingrained vanished. He summed up what happened, and how it applies to humans:

> Different conditions productive of extreme excitation often lead to profound and prolonged loss of balance in nervous and psychic activity . . . neuroses and psychoses may develop as a result of extreme danger to oneself or to near friends, or even the spectacle of some frightful event not affecting one directly.

People tend to have short memories. Most of the time they can forget about bad experiences and fail to heed lessons previously learned.

But hard-core stress leaves a scar.

Experiencing something that makes you stare ruin in the face and question whether you'll survive can permanently reset your expectations and change behaviors that were previously ingrained.

"A mind that is stretched by new experience can never go back to its old dimensions," said Oliver Wendell Holmes.

It's why the generation who lived through the Great Depression never viewed money the same afterward. They saved more money, took on less debt, and were wary of risk—for the rest of their lives. This was obvious even before the Depression was over. Frederick Lewis Allen quotes a *Fortune* magazine article written in 1936:

> The present-day college generation is fatalistic . . . it will not stick its neck out. It keeps its pants buttoned, its chin up, and its mouth shut. If we take the mean average to be the truth, it is a cautious, subdued, unadventurous generation.

Same thing after World War II.

The postwar years saw an economic boom in the United States. Europe, physically destroyed, was a different story. In 1947 Hamilton Fish Armstrong reported in *Foreign Affairs* magazine about life in Europe:

> Every minute is dedicated to scrounging enough food, clothing and fuel to carry through the next 24 hours. There is too little of everything . . . too few houses to live in and not enough glass to supply them with window panes; too little leather for shoes, wool for sweaters, gas for cooking, cotton for diapers, sugar for jam, fats for frying, milk for babies, soap for washing.

After the war, John Maynard Keynes predicted countries wrecked by war would go on to have a "craving for social and personal security."

Which is what happened.

Historian Tony Judt notes that the state of affairs was so bad in postwar Europe that only the state could offer hope of salvation to the masses of displaced people. So it did. Everything from generous unemployment insurance to universal health care became common after the war in ways that never caught on in America.

Historian Michael Howard has said that war and welfare go hand in hand. Perhaps that's because even the most financially prepared, the most risk averse, and those with the most foresight can be completely crushed by war. Europeans did not get to choose whether they wanted to be caught up in World War II— it became the most pressing issue of their lives whether they supported it or not, and it crushed their sense of control whether they prepared for it or not.

It's why baby boomers who lived through the 1970s and '80s think about inflation in ways their children couldn't fathom as young adults.

And it's why you can separate today's tech entrepreneurs into two clearly different buckets—those who experienced the dot-com crash in the late 1990s, and those who didn't because they were too young.

Two things tend to happen after you get hit with something big and unexpected:

- You assume what just happened will keep happening, but with greater force and consequence.
- You forecast with great conviction, despite the original event being improbable and something few, if anyone, predicted.

The more impactful the surprise, the more this is true.

And, importantly, the more those who didn't experience that big event will struggle to understand your point of view.

The oldest story is that of two sides who don't agree with each other.

The question "Why don't you agree with me?" can have infinite answers. Sometimes one side is selfish, or stupid, or blind, or uninformed.

But usually a better question is, "What have you experienced that I haven't that makes you believe what you do? And would I think about the world like you do if I experienced what you have?"

It's the question that contains the most answers about why people don't agree with one another.

But it's such a hard question to ask.

It's uncomfortable to think that what you haven't experienced might change what you believe, because it's admitting your own ignorance. It's much easier to assume that those who disagree with you aren't thinking as hard as you are.

So people will disagree, even as access to information explodes. They may disagree more than ever because, as Benedict Evans says, "The more the Internet exposes people to new points of view, the angrier people get that different views exist."

Disagreement has less to do with what people know and more to do with what they've experienced.

And since experiences will always be different, disagreement will be constant.

Same as it's ever been.

Same as it will always be.

Same as it ever was.

Questions

THE NIGHT BEFORE the D-Day invasion, Franklin Roosevelt asked his wife, Eleanor, how she felt about not knowing what would happen next.

"To be nearly sixty and still rebel at uncertainty is ridiculous isn't it?" she said.

It is. But we do. We always have. We always will.

The idea that what lies in front of us is a dark hole of uncertainty can be so intimidating, it's easier to believe the opposite—that we can see the future, and that its path is logical and predictable. No belief in history is as commonly held, and no belief is as consistently wrong.

The typical attempt to clear up an uncertain future is to gaze further and squint harder—to forecast with more precision, more data, and more intelligence.

Far more effective is to do the opposite: Look backward, and be broad. Rather than attempting to figure out little ways the future might change, study the big things the past has never avoided.

A decade ago I made a goal to read more history and fewer forecasts. It was one of the most enlightening changes of my life. And the irony is that the more history I read, the more comfortable I became with the future. When you focus on what never changes, you stop trying to predict uncertain events and spend more time understanding timeless behavior. Hopefully this book nudged you down that path.

I try not to give advice to people I don't know, because everyone's different and universal guidance is rare.

So rather than ending this book with a list of conclusions to implement in your own life, I'll leave you with a list of questions, all related to the chapters you just read, to ask yourself.

Who has the right answers but I ignore because they're not articulate?

Which of my current views would I disagree with if I were born in a different country or generation?

What do I desperately want to be true so much that I think it's true when it's clearly not?

What is a problem that I think applies only to other countries/industries/careers that will eventually hit me?

What do I think is true but is actually just good marketing?

What haven't I experienced firsthand that leaves me naive about how something works?

What looks unsustainable but is actually a new trend we haven't accepted yet?

Who do I think is smart but is actually full of it?

Am I prepared to handle risks I can't even envision?

Which of my current views would change if my incentives were different?

What are we ignoring today that will seem shockingly obvious in the future?

What events very nearly happened that would have fundamentally changed the world I know if they had occurred?

How much have things outside my control contributed to things I take credit for?

How do I know if I'm being patient (a skill) or stubborn (a flaw)?

Who do I look up to that is secretly miserable?

What hassle am I trying to eliminate that's actually an unavoidable cost of success?

What crazy genius that I aspire to emulate is actually just crazy?

What strong belief do I hold that's most likely to change?

What's always been true?

What's the same as ever?

Acknowledgments

Writing can be a lonely endeavor. It's just you, the keyboard, and a brain that floats between exciting creativity one moment and doubt the next.

But in some ways the profession is social at its core. Every writer can reflect on how many people they've been inspired by, and recognize the dozens or hundreds of other writers, thinkers, researchers, and diverse minds their writing has been shaped by.

A few who have been particularly inspirational and helpful to me, whether they know it or not:

Carl Richards

John Reeves

Craig Shapiro

Dan Gardner

Bethany McLean

Kathleen Kimball

Matt Koppenheffer

Jason Zweig

Betty Cossitt

Noah Schwartzberg

Mollie Glick

Mark Pingle

Craig Pearce

Brian Richards

Jenna Abdou

Mike Ehrlich

Erik Larson

Bill Mann

Derek Thompson

Tom Gaynor

Chris Hill

Candice Millard

Robert Kurson

Jung-ju Kim

James Clear

Frank Housel Sr.

Michael Batnick

And of course, my wife, Gretchen, and my parents, Ben and Nancy—whose support and guidance I'd be lost without.

Notes

Epigraphs

xi **"Our life is indeed the same":** Carl Jung, *Collected Works of C. G. Jung, vol. 7: Two Essays in Analytical Psychology* (Princeton, NJ, Princeton University Press, 1972).

xi **"The wise in all ages":** Arthur Schopenhauer, *The Wisdom of Life, Being the First Part of Arthur Schopenhauer's Aphorismen Zur Lebensweisheit* (London: S. Sonnenschein & Co., 1897).

xi **"I've learned an important trick":** Tim Ferriss, *Tools of Titans: The Tactics, Routines, and Habits of Billionaires, Icons, and World-Class Performers* (Boston: Houghton Mifflin Harcourt, 2017).

xi **"The dead outnumber the living":** Niall Ferguson, *Civilization: The West and the Rest* (New York: Penguin Books, 2012).

Introduction

2 **Amazon founder Jeff Bezos:** Jeff Hayden, "20 Years Ago, Jeff Bezos Said This 1 Thing Separates People Who Achieve Lasting Success From Those Who Don't," *Inc.*, November 6, 2017, www.inc.com /jeff-haden/20-years-ago-jeff-bezos-said-this-1-thing-separates -people-who-achieve-lasting-success-from-those-who-dont.html.

3 **Entrepreneur and investor Naval Ravikant:** Eric Jorgenson, *The Almanack of Naval Ravikant: A Guide to Wealth and Happiness* (N.p.: Magrathea, 2020), 82.

Hanging by a Thread

5 **Author Tim Urban once wrote:** Tim Urban, @waitbutwhy, Twitter post, April 21, 2021, 1:13 p.m., twitter.com/waitbutwhy /status/1384963403475791872?s=20&t=4i2ekW6c1cwAp6S1qB6YUA.

11 **Historian David McCullough:** *Charlie Rose*, season 14, episode 186, "David McCullough," May 30, 2005, PBS, charlierose.com /videos/18134.

11 **Compelled to save money:** Erik Larson, *Dead Wake: The Last Crossing of the Lusitania* (New York: Crown, 2015), 117, 326.

12 **Zangara fired five shots:** Joseph T. McCann, *Terrorism on American Soil* (Boulder, CO: Sentient Publications, 2006), 69–70.

12 **The target, Franklin Delano Roosevelt:** "This Day in History: February 15, 1933: FDR Escapes Assassination Attempt in Miami," History.com, November 16, 2009, updated February 11, 2021, history.com/this-day-in-history/fdr-escapes-assassination-in-miami.

Risk Is What You Don't See

16 **As Prather descended:** Douglas Brinkley, *American Moonshot* (New York: Harper, 2019), 237.

16 **While connecting himself:** Jan Herman, "Stratolab: The Navy's High-Altitude Balloon Research," lecture, Naval Medical Research Institute, Bethesda, MD, 1995, archive.org/details /StratolabTheNavysHighAltitudeBalloonResearch.

16 **As financial advisor Carl Richards says:** Carl Richards, (@behaviorgap), Twitter post, March 10, 2020, 8:19 a.m., twitter .com/behaviorgap/status/1237352317592076288.

17 **In October 1929:** "Fisher Sees Stocks Permanently High," *New York Times*, October 16, 1929, www.nytimes.com/1929/10/16/archives /fisher-sees-stocks-permanently-high-yale-economist-tells -purchasing.html.

17 **I asked Robert Shiller:** Author interview with Robert Shiller, 2012.

19 **the biggest problem of the United States:** Frederick Lewis Allen, *Since Yesterday* (New York: Harper & Brothers, 1940), reproduced from Thurman W. Arnold, *The Folklore of Capitalism* (New Haven, CT: Yale University Press, 1937).

19 **"I'm thinking of all the historians":** Margaret MacMillan, *History's People: Personalities and the Past* (CBC Massey Lectures) (Toronto: House of Anansi Press, 2015).

20 **There's a haunting video:** "The Sonic Memorial—Remembering 9/11 with Host Paul Auster," n.d., in *The Kitchen Sisters* (podcast), kitchensisters.org/present/sonic-memorial/.

21 **"Invest in preparedness":** Nassim Nicholas Taleb, *Antifragile: Things That Gain from Disorder* (New York: Random House, 2014).

Expectations and Reality

24 **"The present and immediate future":** "Where Do We Go from Here?," *Life*, January 5, 1953, 86, books.google.com/books?id=QUIEAAAAMBAJ&q=astonishingly#v=snippet&q=astonishingly&f=false.

24 **"10 straight years":** "What Have We Got Here," *Life*, January 5, 1953, 47, https://books.google.com/books?id=QUIEAAAAMBAJ&q=astonishingly#v=onepage&q=straight%20years&f=false.

24 **George Friedman, a geopolitical forecaster:** "The Crisis of the Middle Class and American Power," RANE Worldview, December 31, 2013, worldview.stratfor.com/article/crisis-middle-class-and-american-power.

25 **Median family income adjusted for inflation:** Russell Sage Foundation, Chartbook of Social Inequality, "Real Mean and Median Income, Families and Individuals, 1947–2012, and Households, 1967–2012," n.d., russellsage. org/sites/all/files/chartbook/Income%20and%20Earnings.pdf.

25 **$29,000 in 1955:** Jessica Semega and Melissa Kollar, "Income in the United States: 2021," U.S. Census Bureau, Report Number P60-276, September 13, 2022, census.gov/library/publications/2022/demo/p60-276.html#:~:text=Real%20median%20household%20income%20was,and%20Table%20A%2D1).

25 **Median hourly wages:** Lawrence H. Officer and Samuel H. Williamson, "Annual Wages in the United States, 1774—Present," MeasuringWorth, 2023, measuringworth.com/datasets/uswage/result.php.

25 **The homeownership rate:** PK, "Historical Homeownership Rate in the United States, 1890–Present," DQYDJ, n.d., dqydj.com /historical-homeownership-rate-united-states.

25 **An average home was a third smaller:** Maria Cecilia P. Moura, Steven J. Smith, and David B. Belzer, "120 Years of U.S. Residential Housing Stock and Floor Space," table 1, *PLoS One* 10, no. 8 (August 11, 2015): e0134135, ncbi.nlm.nih.gov/pmc/articles/PMC4532357 /table/pone.0134135.t001.

25 **Food consumed 29 percent:** U.S. Bureau of Labor Statistics, "100 Years of U.S. Consumer Spending," Report 991, May 2006, bls.gov /opub/100-years-of-u-s-consumer-spending.pdf, and "Consumer Expenditures—2021," news release, September 8, 2022, bls.gov /news.release/cesan.nr0.htm.

26 **Workplace deaths were three times higher:** Marian L. Tupy, "Workplace Fatalities Fell 95% in the 20th Century. Who Deserves the Credit?," FEE Stories, September 16, 2018, fee.org/articles/workplace -fatalities-fell-95-in-the-20th-century-who-deserves-the-credit.

26 **But Ferencz said none of it:** Barry Avrich, *Prosecuting Evil* (Los Angeles: Vertical Entertainment, 2018).

26 *The New York Times* **interviewed Gary Kremen:** Gary Rivlin, "In Silicon Valley, Millionaires Who Don't Feel Rich," *New York Times*, August 5, 2007, https://www.nytimes.com/2007/08/05/technology /05rich.html.

29 **Actor Will Smith:** Will Smith, *Will* (New York: Penguin Press, 2021), 105.

30 **Tennis player Naomi Osaka:** Steve Tignor, "Naomi Osaka Isn't Enjoying Herself Even When She Wins—So You Can Understand Her Need for a Break from the Game," *Tennis*, September 4, 2021, tennis.com/news/ articles/naomi-osaka-isn-t-enjoying-herself-even -when-she-wins-so-you-can-understand-her-.

30 **"We should be less than candid":** David McCullough, *Truman* (New York: Touchstone, 1992).

31 **"You seem extremely happy":** Buffett Online, "2022 Daily Journal Annual Meeting," February 16, 2022, YouTube video, youtube.com /watch?v=22faKkazye4&ab_channel=BuffettOnline.

Wild Minds

33 **He and two other runners:** Cathal Dennehy, "Eliud Kipchoge: Inside the Camp, and the Mind, of the Greatest Marathon Runner of All Time," *Irish Examiner*, October 29, 2021, irishexaminer.com /sport/othersport/arid-40732662.html.

34 **John Boyd was probably the greatest:** Robert Coram, *Boyd: The Fighter Pilot Who Changed the Art of War* (New York: Back Bay Books, 2004), 58, 68, 130, 172, 450.

35 **Boyd is known:** Ronald Spector, "40-Second Man," review of *Boyd: The Fighter Pilot Who Changed the Art of War, New York Times*, March 9, 2003, nytimes.com/2003/03/09/books/40-second-man.html.

35 **"This brilliant young officer":** Coram, *Boyd*, 184.

36 **"I have glanced through a great quantity":** John Maynard Keynes, "Newton, the Man," undelivered lecture, in Elizabeth Johns, ed., *The Collected Writings of John Maynard Keynes* (Cambridge and London: Cambridge University Press and Royal Economic Society, 1978), available at mathshistory.st-andrews.ac.uk/Extras/Keynes_Newton.

36 **There's a scene in the movie** *Patton*: Franklin J. Schaffner *Patton* (Los Angeles: 20th Century Fox, 1970).

37 **constantly dropping nuclear bombs:** Loren Grush, "Elon Musk Elaborates on His Proposal to Nuke Mars," Verge, October 2, 2015, theverge.com/2015/10/2/9441029/elon-musk-mars-nuclear-bomb -colbert-interview-explained.

37 **humanity is a computer simulation:** Andrew Griffin, "Elon Musk: The Chance We Are Not Living in a Computer Simulation Is 'One in Billions,'" *Independent*, June 2, 2016, independent.co.uk/tech /elon-musk-ai-artificial-intelligence-computer-simulation-gaming -virtual-reality-a7060941.html.

39 **Naval Ravikant once wrote:** Eric Jorgenson, *The Almanack of Naval Ravikant: A Guide to Wealth and Happiness* (N.p.: Magrathea, 2020), 144.

Wild Numbers

40 **Jerry Seinfeld was once driving:** *Comedians in Cars Getting Coffee*, season 5, episodes 7–8, "The Unsinkable Legend—Part 1 & Part 2," December 18, 2014, Crackle.

41 **the movie *Zero Dark Thirty*:** Kathryn Bigelow, *Zero Dark Thirty* (Culver City, CA: Sony Pictures, 2012).

42 **After the bin Laden raid:** John A. Gans Jr., "'This Is 50-50': Behind Obama's Decision to Kill Bin Laden," *Atlantic*, October 10, 2012, theatlantic.com/international/archive/2012/10/this-is-50-50 -behind-obamas-decision-to-kill-bin-laden/263449.

43 **Daniel Kahneman once said:** Tim Adams, "This Much I Know: Daniel Kahneman," *Guardian*, July 7, 2012, theguardian.com /science/2012/jul/08/this-much-i-know-daniel-kahneman.

43 **Evelyn Marie Adams won \$3.9 million:** Robert D. McFadden, "Odds-Defying Jersey Woman Hits Lottery Jackpot 2d Time," *New York Times*, February 14, 1986, nytimes.com/1986/02/14/nyregion /odds-defying-jersey-woman-hits-lottery-jackpot-2d-time.html.

43 **figured it was 1 in 30:** Gina Kolata, "1-in-a-Trillion Coincidence, You Say? Not Really, Experts Find," *New York Times*, February 27, 1990, nytimes. com/1990/02/27/science/1-in-a-trillion-coincidence -you-say-not-really-experts-find.html.

44 **Physicist Freeman Dyson:** Freeman Dyson, "One in a Million," *New York Review of Books*, March 25, 2004, nybooks.com/articles /2004/03/25/one-in-a-million.

45 **describes how Americans stayed informed:** Frederick Lewis Allen, *The Big Change: American Transforms Itself 1900–1950* (1952; rept., New York: Routledge, 2017), 8, 23.

46 **Eighteen hundred U.S. print media outlets:** Megan Garber, "The Threat to American Democracy That Has Nothing to Do with Trump," *Atlantic*, July 11, 2020, theatlantic.com/culture/archive /2020/07/ghosting-news-margaret-sullivans-alarm-bell/614011.

46 **steadily more gloomy:** Steven Pinker, "The Media Exaggerates Negative News. This Distortion Has Consequences," *Guardian*, February 17, 2018, theguardian.com/commentisfree/2018/feb/17 /steven-pinker-media-negative-news.

46 **Compare this to the past:** Allen, *The Big Change*, 8.

47 **"The Psychology of Human Misjudgment":** Peter T. Kaufman, ed., *Poor Charlie's Almanack: The Wit and Wisdom of Charles T. Munger* (Marceline, MO: Walsworth Publishing Co., 2005), 205.

48 **Professor Philip Tetlock has spent:** Eric Schurenberg, "Why
the Experts Missed the Crash," CNN Money, February 18, 2009, money.
cnn.com/2009/02/17/pf/experts_Tetlock.moneymag
/index.htm.

48 **But how many recessions:** National Bureau of Economic
Research, "Business Cycle Dating," n.d., nber.org/research
/business-cycle-dating.

Best Story Wins

52 **King's advisor and speechwriter:** *Wall Street Journal*, "How Martin
Luther King Went Off Script in 'I Have a Dream,'" August 24, 2013,
YouTube video, youtube.com/watch?v=KxlOlynG6FY.

52 **The first few minutes of King's speech:** Martin Luther King Jr., "I Have
a Dream," speech given at March on Washington for Jobs and Freedom,
Washington, D.C., August 28, 1963, transcript at americanrhetoric.com/
speeches/mlkihaveadream.htm.

52 **gospel singer Mahalia Jackson:** "This Day in History: August 28, 1963:
Mahalia Jackson Prompts Martin Luther King Jr. to Improvise 'I Have a
Dream' Speech," History.com, n.d., history.com/this-day
-in-history/mahalia-jackson-the-queen-of-gospel-puts-her-stamp-on
-the-march-on-washington.

52 **King looks up:** King, "I Have a Dream," youtube.com/watch?v
=smEqnnklfYs.

53 **Mark Twain was perhaps:** Ken Burns, *Mark Twain* (Walpole,
NH, and Arlington, VA: Florentine Films in association with WETA,
2001).

53 **C. R. Hallpike is an anthropologist:** C. R. Hallpike, "Review of Yuval
Harari's Sapiens: A Brief History of Humankind," AIPavilion, 2017,
aipavilion.github.io/docs/hallpike-review.pdf.

54 **Harari once said about writing** *Sapiens:* Ian Parker, "Yuval Noah Harari's
History of Everyone, Ever," *New Yorker*, February 10, 2020, newyorker.
com/magazine/2020/02/17/yuval-noah-harari-gives-the
-really-big-picture.

54 **But in 1990 Ken Burns's:** Ken Burns, *The Civil War* (Walpole, NH, and
Arlington, VA: Florentine Films in association with WETA, 1990).

55 **Burns once described:** "Ken Burns," *SmartLess* (podcast), September 20, 2021, podcasts.apple.com/us/podcast/ken-burns /id1521578868?i=1000535978926.

56 **Chinese ferryboat *SS Kiangya*:** Mfame Team, "The Tragedy of SS Kiangya," Mfame, January 21, 2016, mfame.guru/tragedy-ss-kiangya.

56 **MV *Dona Paz*:** Editorial Team, "Sinking of Doña Paz: The World's Deadliest Shipping Accident," Safety4Sea, March 8, 2022, safety4sea .com/cm-sinking-of-dona-paz-the-worlds-deadliest-shipping-accident.

56 **MV *Le Joola*:** "'Africa's Titanic' 20 Years Later: Sinking of Le Joola Has Lessons for Ferry Safety," SaltWire, October 3, 2022, saltwire .com/halifax/news/local/africas-titanic-20-years-later-sinking-of -le-joola-has-lessons-for-ferry-safety-100778847.

57 **"Humor is a way to show":** Ken Burns, *Mark Twain*.

58 **Richard Feynman, an astounding storyteller:** "Richard Feynman Fire," Nebulajr, April 15, 2009, YouTube video, youtube.com /watch?v=N1pIYI5JQLE&ab_channel=nebulajr.

58 **Part of what made:** Walter Isaacson, *Einstein: His Life and Universe* (New York: Simon & Schuster, 2007).

59 **Steven Spielberg noted this:** Anthony Breznican, "Steven Spielberg: The EW interview," *Entertainment Weekly*, December 2, 2011, ew.com/article/2011/12/02/steven-spielberg -ew-interview.

60 **Visa founder Dee Hock:** Dee Hock, *Autobiography of a Restless Mind: Reflections on the Human Condition*, vol. 2 (Bloomington, IN: iUniverse, 2013).

Does Not Compute

61 **"Logic is an invention of man":** Will Durant, *Fallen Leaves: Last Words on Life, Love, War, and God* (New York: Simon & Schuster, 2014).

62 **He said something was missing:** Ken Burns and Lynn Novick, *The Vietnam War* (Walpole, NH: Florentine Films et al., 2017).

62 **"We're killing these people":** Burns and Novick, *The Vietnam War*.

63 **Carved on the wall:** Ron Baker, "The McKinsey Maxim: 'What You Can Measure You Can Manage.' HOKUM!," Firm of the Future, February 18, 2020, firmofthefuture.com/content/the-mckinsey-maxim-what-you-can-measure-you-can-manage-hokum.

63 **Jeff Bezos once said:** Julie Bort, "Amazon Founder Jeff Bezos Explains
Why He Sends Single Character '?' Emails," *Inc.*, April 23, 2018, inc.com/
business-insider/amazon-founder-ceo-jeff-bezos
-customer-emails-forward-managers-fix-issues.html.

64 **An aide to Bradley:** Niall Ferguson, *The War of the World: Twentieth-
Century Conflict and the Descent of the West* (New York: Penguin Press,
2006), 537.

64 **Hill, a British physiologist:** The Nobel Prize, "Archibald V. Hill:
Biographical," 1922, nobelprize.org/prizes/medicine/1922/hill
/biographical.

64 **Hill's early work:** Timothy David Noakes, "Fatigue Is a Brain-Derived
Emotion That Regulates the Exercise Behavior to Ensure the Protection
of Whole Body Homeostasis," *Frontiers in Physiology* 3, no. 82 (2012): 1,
ncbi.nlm.nih.gov/pmc/articles/PMC3323922.

65 **Hill's calculations had almost:** Eric R. Kandel, *In Search of Memory: The
Emergence of a New Science of Mind* (New York:
W. W. Norton, 2007).

65 **Hill, once wedded:** Alex Hutchinson, *Endure: Mind, Body, and the
Curiously Elastic Limits of Human Performance* (Boston: Mariner Books,
2018), 22–27 and 45–76.

65 **"To tell you the truth":** "(1) Muscular Movement in Man: The Factors
Governing Speed and Recovery from Fatigue (2) Living Machinery: Six
Lectures Delivered before a 'Juvenile Auditory' at the Royal Institution,
Christmas 1926 (3) Basal Metabolism in Health and Disease," *Nature* 121
(1928): 314–16, nature.com/articles/121314a0.

Calm Plants the Seeds of Crazy

72 **Minsky's seminal theory:** Hyman P. Minsky, "The Financial Instability
Hypothesis," Working Paper No. 74, Levy Economics Institute of Bard
College, May 1992, levyinstitute.org/pubs/wp74.pdf.

74 **"Everything feels unprecedented":** Kelly Hayes,
@MsKellyMHayes, Twitter post, July 11, 2020, 4:22 p.m., twitter
.com/MsKellyMHayes/status/1282093046943952902.

74 **Historian Dan Carlin:** Dan Carlin, *The End Is Always Near*
(New York: Harper, 2019), 194.

74 **decline in infectious disease:** Victoria Hansen et al., "Infectious Disease Mortality Trends in the United States, 1980–2014," *Journal of the American Medical Association* 316, no. 20 (November 22/29, 2016): 2149–51. https://jamanetwork.com/journals/jama/article-abstract/2585966.

75 **Clark Whelton, a former speechwriter:** Clark Whelton, "Say Your Prayers and Take Your Chances," *City Journal*, March 13, 2020, city-journal.org/1957-asian-flu-pandemic.

76 **Lori Freeman, CEO:** Ed Yong, "How the Pandemic Defeated America," *Atlantic*, September 2020, theatlantic.com/magazine/archive/2020/09/coronavirus-american-failure/614191.

77 **Parts of Lake Tahoe received:** Admin, "Incredible 2017 Tahoe Snow Totals," *Tahoe Ski World*, December 28, 2018, tahoeskiworld.com/incredible-2017-tahoe-snow-totals.

77 **It was called a superbloom:** Associated Press, "Out in the California Desert, Tourists Make a Beeline for 'Flowergeddon,'" *Washington Post*, March 31, 2017, washingtonpost.com/lifestyle/kidspost/out-of-the-california-desert-tourists-make-a-beeline-for-flowergeddon/2017/03/31/64313c3c-1620-11e7-833c-503e1f6394c9_story.html.

77 **"A wet year reduces fires":** S.-Y. Simon Wang, "How Might El Niño Affect Wildfires in California?," *ENSO* (blog), August 27, 2014, climate.gov/news-features/blogs/enso/how-might-el-ni%C3%B1o-affect-wildfires-california.

79 **Investor Chamath Palihapitiya:** "Chamath Palihapitiya: The #1 Secret to Becoming Rich," Investor Center, February 5, 2021, YouTube video, youtube.com/watch?v=XnleEVXdQsE&ab_channel=InvestorCenter.

Too Much, Too Soon, Too Fast

82 **J. B. S. Haldane once showed:** J. B. S. Haldane, "On Being the Right Size," in *Possible Worlds and Other Essays* (London: Chatto & Windus, 1927), 18, available at searchworks.stanford.edu/view/8708294.

82 **Here's how often the U.S. stock market:** Robert J. Shiller, "Online Data Robert Shiller," http://www.econ.yale.edu/~shiller/data.htm.

83 **Howard Schultz wrote to senior management:** Howard Schultz, memo to Jim Donald, February 14, 2007, starbucksgossip.typepad.com/_/2007/02/starbucks_chair_2.html.

84 **Tire tycoon Harvey Firestone:** Harvey S. Firestone, *Men and Rubber: The Story of Business* (New York: Doubleday, Page & Co., 1926), available at https://blas.com/wp-content/uploads/2019/07/Men-and-Rubber.pdf.

85 **"A tree that grows quickly rots quickly":** Peter Wohlleben, *The Secret Wisdom of Nature* (Vancouver: Greystone Books, 2019).

86 **That's what a team of biologists:** Who-Seung Lee, Pat Monaghan, and Neil B. Metcalfe, "Experimental Demonstration of the Growth Rate–Lifespan Trade-off," *Proceedings of the Royal Society B* 280 (2013): 20122370, royalsocietypublishing.org/doi/pdf/10.1098/rspb.2012.2370.

When the Magic Happens

87 **The Triangle Shirtwaist Factory fire:** Ric Burns, *New York: A Documentary Film* (New York: Steeplechase Films and New York: New-York Historical Society et al., 1999–2003).

88 **"Thud-dead, thud-dead, thud-dead":** William Shepherd, "Eyewitness at the Triangle," in *Out of the Sweatshop: The Struggle for Industrial Democracy*, ed. Leon Stein (New York: Quadrangle/New Times Book Company, 1977), 188–93, available at trianglefire.ilr.cornell.edu/primary/testimonials/ootss_WilliamShepherd.html.

92 **the burst of scientific progress:** Frederick Lewis Allen, *The Big Change: American Transforms Itself 1900–1950* (1952; rept., New York: Routledge, 2017).

92 **Shopify founder Toby Lütke:** Brad Stone, "How Shopify Outfoxed Amazon to Become the Everywhere Store," *Bloomberg*, December 22, 2021, bloomberg.com/news/features/2021-12-23/shopify-amazon-retail-rivalry-heats-up-with-covid-sparked-online-shopping-booma.

93 **Economist Alex Field:** Alexander J. Field, *A Great Leap Forward: 1930s Depression and U.S. Economic Growth* (New Haven, CT: Yale University Press, 2012), 7.

94 **The Department of Highway Transportation:** Federal Highway Administration, "Contributions and Crossroads: Timeline," n.d., fhwa.dot.gov/candc/timeline.cfm.

94 **Franklin Roosevelt said in a speech:** Franklin D. Roosevelt, "Campaign Address in Portland, Oregon on Public Utilities and Development of Hydro-Electric Power," September 21, 1932, available at presidency.ucsb.edu/documents/campaign-address-portland-oregon-public-utilities-and-development-hydro-electric-power.

96 **Robert Gordon wrote:** Robert Gordon, *The Rise and Fall of American Growth* (Princeton, NJ: Princeton University Press, 2016), 564.

97 **Richard Nixon once observed:** JM, "The Purpose of Life: Nixon," July 9, 2011, YouTube video, youtube.com/watch?v=Pc3IfB23W4c&ab_channel=JM.

98 **Entrepreneur Andrew Wilkinson:** Andrew Wilkinson, @awilkinson, Twitter post, April 26, 2021, 8:07 a.m., twitter.com /awilkinson/status/1386698431905730565?s=20.

98 **Investor Patrick O'Shaughnessy:** Patrick O'Shaughnessy, @patrick _oshag, Twitter post, July 17, 2021, 6:31 a.m., twitter.com/patrick _oshag/status/1416390114998198273?s=20&t=n2YwiLib6570_69Iyprf7g.

Overnight Tragedies and Long-Term Miracles

100 **Dwight Eisenhower ate a hamburger:** Cody White, "'Heart Attack Strikes Ike,' President Eisenhower's 1955 Medical Emergency in Colorado," National Archives, September 22, 2016, text-message .blogs.archives.gov/2016/09/22/heart-attack-strikes-ike-president -eisenhowers-1955-medical-emergency-in-colorado.

101 **Historian David Wooton:** Nassim Nicholas Taleb, *Antifragile: Things That Gain from Disorder* (New York: Random House, 2014).

Tiny and Magnificent

105 **A 2010 Yale study showed:** Marc Santore, "Study Finds Snacking Is a Major Cause of Child Obesity," Yale School of Medicine, April 2, 2010, medicine.yale.edu/news-article/study-finds-snacking-is-a -major-cause-of-child-obesity.

106 **"The island over which the explosion took place":** Dan Carlin, *The End Is Always Near* (New York: Harper, 2019), 148.

106 **One, called Davy Crockett:** Matthew Seelinger, "The M28/M29 Davy Crockett Nuclear Weapon System," Army Historical Foundation, armyhistory.org/the-m28m29-davy-crockett-nuclear-weapon-system.

107 **Cuban Missile Crisis:** Serhii Plokhy, *Nuclear Folly: A History of the Cuban Missile Crisis* (New York: W. W. Norton, 2021).

108 **Tenerife airport disaster:** Niall Ferguson, *Doom: The Politics of Catastrophe* (London: Penguin Books, 2021), 258–62.

109 **Biologist Leslie Orgel:** Jack D. Dunitz and Gerald F. Joyce, "A Biographical Memoir of Leslie E. Orgel, 1927–2007" (Washington, D.C.: National Academy of Sciences, 2013), nasonline.org/publications/biographical-memoirs/memoir-pdfs/orgel-leslie.pdf.

110 **Investor Howard Marks:** "Howard Marks—Embracing the Psychology of Investing," June 21, 2021, in *Invest Like the Best with Patrick O'Shaughnessy* (podcast), joincolossus.com/episodes/70790270/marks-embracing-the-psychology-of-investing?tab=transcript.

Elation and Despair

112 **Stockdale was asked in an interview:** Jim Collins, "The Stockdale Paradox," JimCollins.com, jimcollins.com/media_topics/TheStockdaleParadox.html.

113 **"The American dream":** James Truslow Adams, *The Epic of America* (1931; rept., New York: Routledge, 2017).

114 **Jane Pauley interviewed:** CNBC Make It, "Bill Gates Wasn't Worried about Burnout in 1984—Here's Why," February 25, 2019, YouTube video, youtube.com/watch?v=MhnSzwXvGfc&ab_channel=CNBCMakeIt.

114 **the first time he met Bill:** Paul Allen, *Idea Man* (New York: Portfolio/Penguin, 2011), 32.

114 **From the day he started:** Leah Fessler, "Bill Gates' Biggest Worry as a 31-Year-Old Billionaire Wasn't Apple or IBM," Yahoo! News, February 28, 2018, yahoo.com/news/bill-gates-biggest-worry-31-170014556.html.

Casualties of Perfection

118 **a Russian biologist:** Georgy S. Levit, Uwe Hossfeld, and Lennart Olsson, "From the 'Modern Synthesis' to Cybernetics: Ivan Ivanovich Schmalhausen (1884–1963) and His Research Program for a Synthesis of Evolutionary and Developmental Biology," *Journal of Experimental Zoology Part B: Molecular and Developmental Evolution* 306, no. 2 (March 15, 2006): 89–106, pubmed.ncbi.nlm.nih.gov/16419076.

118 **become very good at one thing:** Richard Lewontin and Richard Levins, "Schmalhausen's Law," *Capitalism Nature Socialism* 11, no. 4 (2000): 103–8, tandfonline.com/doi/abs/10.1080/10455750009358943?journalCode=rcns20.

119 **Secretary of State George Shultz:** David Leonhardt, "You're Too Busy. You Need a 'Shultz Hour,'" *New York Times*, April 18, 2017, nytimes.com/2017/04/18/opinion/youre-too-busy-you-need-a-shultz-hour.html.

120 **walking increases creativity:** May Wong, "Stanford Study Finds Walking Improves Creativity," Stanford News, April 24, 2014, news.stanford.edu/2014/04/24/walking-vs-sitting-042414.

120 **Warren Buffett's secret was:** Charlie Munger, "2007 USC Law School Commencement Address," University of Southern California Law School, Los Angeles, CA, May 13, 2007, jamesclear.com/great-speeches/2007-usc-law-school-commencement-address-by-charlie-munger.

121 **Nassim Taleb says, "My only measure":** Nassim Nicholas Taleb, *The Bed of Procrustes* (New York: Random House, 2010), 37.

It's Supposed to Be Hard

124 **Few stories make you wince:** Ric Burns, *The Donner Party* (New York: Steeplechase Films, 1992).

125 *Lawrence of Arabia*: David Lean, *Lawrence of Arabia* (Culver City, CA: Columbia Pictures, 1962).

126 **"The safest way to try":** Shane Parrish, "Simple Acts," *Brain Food* (blog), October 23, 2022, https://fs.blog/brain-food/october-23-2022.

126 **David Letterman asked:** *Comedians in Cars Getting Coffee*, season 2, episode 2, "I Like Kettlecorn," June 20, 2013, Crackle.

127 *Harvard Business Review* **once pointed out:** Daniel McGinn, "Life's Work: An Interview with Jerry Seinfeld," *Harvard Business Review*, January-February 2007, hbr.org/2017/01/lifes-work-jerry-seinfeld.

127 **Jeff Bezos once talked about:** "This Is Killing Your Success: Jeff Bezos," The Outcome, February 14, 2021, YouTube video, youtube.com/watch?v=sbhYoEyOcqg&ab_channel=TheOutcome.

128 **"They couldn't hold a job because":** "Steven Pressfield—How to Overcome Self-Sabotage and Resistance, Routines for Little Successes, and the Hero's Journey vs. the Artist's Journey," February 26, 2021, *The Tim Ferriss Show* (podcast), episode 501, podcasts.apple.com/us/podcast/501-steven-pressfield-how-to-overcome-self-sabotage/id863897795?i=1000510784746.

129 **"If you can't use your legs":** Doris Kearns Goodwin, *No Ordinary Time* (New York: Simon & Schuster, 2008), 218.

Keep Running

131 **later deemed Cope's Rule:** Henry Fairfield Osborn, "A Biographical Memoir of Edward Drinker Cope, 1840–1897" (Washington, D.C.: National Academy of Sciences, 1930).

132 **"The tendency for evolution":** Santa Fe Institute, "Bigger Is Better, Until You Go Extinct," news release, July 21, 2008, santafe.edu /news-center/news/bigger-is-better-until-you-go-extinct.

132 **An ant can fall:** April Holladay, "Ant's Slow Fall Key to Survival," *Globe and Mail* (Toronto), January 12, 2009, theglobeandmail.com /technology/ants-slow-fall-key-to-survival/article4275684.

132 **Big animals also require:** Morgan Housel, "Crickets: The Epitome of Investing Success," Medium, March 10, 2016, medium.com/@TMF Housel/crickets-the-epitome-of-investing-success-9f3bccd2628.

133 **"No one has to tell you":** Isadore Barmash, "A Sears 'Store of the Future,'" Market Place, *New York Times*, July 27, 1983, nytimes.com /1983/07/27/business/market-place-a-sears-store-of-the-future.html.

133 **The *Times* wrote in 1974:** Peter T. Kilborn, "Regan Bids Wall Street Seek Sears's Efficiency," *New York Times*, June 11, 1974, nytimes.com /1974/06/11/archives/regan-bids-wall-street-seek-searss-efficiency2 -unmitigated.html.

134 **lost all their value:** Morgan Housel, "Risk Is How Much Time You Need," Collab Fund, March 30, 2017, collabfund.com/blog/risk.

136 **Van Valen argued:** Leigh Van Valen, "A New Evolutionary Law," *Evolutionary Theory* 1 (July 1973): 1–30, mn.uio.no/cees/english /services/van-valen/evolutionary-theory/volume-1/vol-1-no-1-pages -1-30-l-van-valen-a-new-evolutionary-law.pdf.

The Wonders of the Future

140 **"America's Thinking Men":** "America's Thinking Men Forecast the Wonders of the Future," *Washington Post,* January 12, 1908.

141 **called an arc lamp:** *American Experience,* season 27, episode 3, "Edison," January 27, 2015, PBS.

142 **Fisher's Fundamental Theorem:** Anya Plutynski, "What Was Fisher's Fundamental Theorem of Natural Selection and What Was It For?," *Studies in History and Philosophy of Science Part C:*

Studies in History and Philosophy of Biological and Biomedical Sciences 37 (2006): 59–82, philsci-archive.pitt.edu/15310/1/FundamentalTheorem.pdf.

144 **the first long-distance wireless:** "January 12—Births—Scientists Born on January 12th," Today in Science History, todayinsci.com/1/1_12.htm.

Harder Than It Looks and Not as Fun as It Seems

145 **"You think your pain":** James Baldwin, "The Doom and Glory of Knowing Who You Are," *Life*, May 24, 1963.

147 **Elon Musk once broke down in tears:** David Gelles et al., "Elon Musk Details 'Excruciating' Personal Toll of Tesla Turmoil," *New York Times*, August 16, 2018, nytimes.com/2018/08/16/business/elon-musk-interview-tesla.html.

Incentives: The Most Powerful Force in the World

150 **Rapper Notorious B.I.G.:** Emmett Malloy, *Biggie: I Got a Story to Tell* (Los Gatos, CA: Netflix, 2021).

150 **Soviet poet Yevgeny Yevtushenko:** Yevgeny Yevtushenko, "Career," Goodreads, goodreads.com/quotes/1265237-career-galileo-the-clergy-maintained-was-a-pernicious-and-stubborn.

152 **One of them explained:** *Drug Lords*, season 2, episode 1, "El Chapo," July 10, 2018, Netflix.

153 **didn't show the spaceship:** "Cult's Telescope Couldn't Find UFO," *Chicago Tribune*, April 1, 1997, chicagotribune.com/news/ct-xpm-1997-04-02-9704020119-story.html.

153 **"Show me a man":** Jill Lepore, *These Truths* (New York: W. W. Norton, 2018), 412–13.

153 **is the career incentive:** Heather Lyu et al., "Overtreatment in the United States," *PLoS One* 12, no. 9 (2017): e0181970, ncbi.nlm.nih.gov/pmc/articles/PMC5587107.

154 **"Maybe you can cut down on that":** *The Daily Show*, season 14, episode 36, "Jim Cramer," March 12, 2009, Comedy Central.

Now You Get It

157 **Marine general named Smedley Butler:** John Edgar Hoover, memo to Mr. Tamm, November 22, 1934, vault.fbi.gov/smedley -butler/Smedley%20Butler%20Part%2001%200f%2002.

157 **sweeping Europe at the time:** "Gen. Butler Bares 'Fascist Plot' to Seize Government by Force," *New York Times*, November 21, 1934, nytimes.com/ 1934/11/21/archives/gen-butler-bares-fascist-plot -to-seize-government-by-force-says.html.

157 **"If you find the right balance":** *Comedians in Cars Getting Coffee*, season 6, episode 5, "That's the Whole Point of Apartheid, Jerry," July 1, 2015, Crackle.

158 **The book *What We Knew*:** Eric A. Johnson and Karl-Heinz Reuband, *What We Knew: Terror, Mass Murder, and Everyday Life in Nazi Germany* (New York: Basic Books, 2006), 156.

158 **Or take Varlam Shalamov:** Varlam Shalamov, "Forty-Five Things I Learned in the Gulag," *Paris Review*, June 12, 2018, theparisreview .org/blog/2018/06/12/forty-five-things-i-learned-in-the-gulag.

159 **"There was no way":** Stephen Ambrose, *Citizen Soldiers* (New York: Simon & Schuster, 1998).

159 **Almost 80 percent of Americans:** Pew Research Center, "Public Trust in Government: 1958–2022," June 6, 2022, pewresearch.org /politics/2022/06/06/public-trust-in-government-1958-2022.

160 **"Teachers do one half":** *Tamborine*, directed by Bo Burnham (Los Gatos, CA: Netflix, 2018).

160 **Michael Collins turned to Neil Armstrong:** Andrew Chaikin, *A Man on the Moon* (New York: Viking, 1994).

Trying Too Hard

168 **"There's a paradox":** Barak Goodman, *Cancer: The Emperor of All Maladies* (Brooklyn, NY: Ark Media, 2015).

169 **MIT cancer researcher Robert Weinberg:** Goodman, *Cancer: The Emperor of All Maladies*.

170 **"Simplicity is the hallmark of truth":** Edsger W. Dijkstra, "The Threats to Computing Science," lecture, ACM 1984 South Central Regional Conference, Austin, TX, November 16–18, 1984,

cs.utexas.edu/users/EWD/transcriptions/EWDo8xx/EWD898
.html.

170 **"The course of evolution has been":** Samuel Wendell Williston, *Water Reptiles of the Past and Present* (Chicago: University of Chicago Press, 1914), archive.org/details/waterreptilesofpoowill/page/172/mode/2up.

171 **Dozens of jawbones:** W. K. Gregory, "Polyisomerism and Anisomerism in Cranial and Dental Evolution among Vertebrates," *Proceedings of the National Academy of Sciences of the United States of America* 20, no. 1 (January 1934): 1–9, semanticscholar.org/paper /Polyisomerism-and-Anisomerism-in-Cranial-and-Dental-Gregory /d683d13e9fbc5ea44b533cb73678c6c2f7941dea?p2dfJordan.

171 **John Reed wrote:** John T. Reed, *Succeeding* (self published: John T. Reed Publishing, 2008).

171 **Stephen King explains:** Stephen King, *On Writing: A Memoir of the Craft* (Scribner: New York, 2000).

173 **quit after a few dozen pages:** Jordan Ellenberg, "The Summer's Most Unread Book Is . . . ," *Wall Street Journal*, July 3, 2014, wsj.com /articles/the-summers-most-unread-book-is-1404417569.

174 **McCrae had never heard of it:** Thomas McCrae, "The Method of Zadig in the Practice of Medicine," Address in Medicine delivered at the annual meeting of the Canadian Medical Association, St. John, NB, July 7, 1914, ncbi.nlm.nih.gov/pmc/articles/PMC406677/pdf /canmedajo0242-0027.pdf.

Wounds Heal, Scars Last

177 **Seventy *thousand* villages were:** Geoffrey Roberts, *Stalin's Wars: From World War to Cold War, 1939–1953* (New Haven, CT: Yale University Press, 2006), 4–5.

177 **only 1,500 calories:** Tokuaki Shobayashi, "History of Nutrition Policy in Japan," *Nutrition Reviews* 78, supp. 3 (December 2020): 10–13, academic.oup.com/nutritionreviews/article/78/Supplement _3/10/6012429.

177 **A study of twenty thousand people:** Rand Corporation, "Lasting Consequences of World War II Means More Illness, Lower Education and Fewer Chances to Marry for Survivors," press release, January 21, 2014, rand.org/news/press/2014/01/21/index1

.html#:~:text=The%20study%20found%20that%20living,more
%20likely%20to%20have%20depression.

178 **"[They] were gnawed at by"**: Frederick Lewis Allen, *The Big Change:
American Transforms Itself 1900–1950* (1952; rept., New York: Routledge,
2017), 148.

179 **Pavlov wrote about:** Ivan P. Pavlov, "Conditioned Reflexes: An
Investigation of the Physiological Activity of the Cerebral Cortex,"
Lecture XVIII, 1927, trans. G. V. Anrep, Classics in the History of
Psychology, March 2001, psychclassics.yorku.ca/Pavlov/lecture18.htm.

179 **how it applies to humans:** Pavlov, "Conditioned Reflexes: An
Investigation of the Physiological Activity of the Cerebral Cortex,"
Lecture XXIII, trans. G. V. Anrep, Classics in the History of Psychology,
July 2001, psychclassics.yorku.ca/Pavlov/lecture23
.htm#:~:text=Different%20conditions%20productive%20of
%20extreme,in%20nervous%20and%20psychic%20activity.

180 **Hamilton Fish Armstrong:** Hamilton Fish Armstrong, "Europe
Revisited," *Foreign Affairs*, July 1947, foreignaffairs.com/articles
/europe/1947-07-01/europe-revisited.

181 **Historian Tony Judt notes:** Tony Judt, *Postwar: A History of Europe Since
1945* (New York: Penguin Press, 2005).

181 **Historian Michael Howard:** Ta-Nehisi Coates, "'War and Welfare
Went Hand in Hand,'" *Atlantic*, November 4, 2013, theatlantic.com/
international/archive/2013/11/war-and-welfare-went-hand-in-hand/281107.

Questions

183 **"To be nearly sixty"**: Doris Kearns Goodwin, *No Ordinary Time* (New
York: Simon & Schuster, 2008).